# Thinking Tactics

A Journey in the Human Mind

# Thinking Tactics

## A Journey in the Human Mind

Mogtaba Elhadi

**Title: Thinking Tactics**
**Author: Mogtaba Mohammed Osman**
Copyright © 2023 by Mogtaba Elhadi



## Disclaimer:

The information provided in this book is intended for educational and informational purposes only. The author and publisher are not offering it as legal, financial, or other professional advice. You should consult with a qualified professional before making any decisions based on the information in this book.

## Trademark Acknowledgments:

All product names, logos, and brands mentioned in this book are the property of their respective owners. Their inclusion does not imply any endorsement, affiliation, or sponsorship by the trademark owners.

## Note:

While every precaution has been taken in the preparation of this book, the publisher and author assume no responsibility for errors or omissions, or for damages resulting from the use of the information contained herein.

## Contacts:

You may reach the author through:
mogtba@gmail.com, or mogtba@mashreq.edu.sd

5

In the name of God, the Entirely Merciful, the Especially Merciful

{And they ask you, about the soul. Say, 'The soul is of the affair of my Lord. And mankind have not been given of knowledge except a little.'}

Holy Quran, Verse (17:85)

Our knowledge will eventually fade,
while thinking techniques will remain.

# Acknowledgment

First and foremost, I thank God for helping me completing and publishing this book. Then to my parents, who have never stopped supporting me in everything I do in my life. To my beloved family, friends, and all those who provided their invaluable opinions and constructive criticism, I extend my heartfelt appreciation. Initially, I started writing this book ten years ago and then stopped, only to abandon it. However, it was my wife who, upon reading one of the thinking patterns, insisted that I dedicate the necessary time and effort to complete it. Hence, she deserves the credit for the emergence of this book.

The greatest gift for any writer lies in having their work read and witnessing its impact on people's lives. This grants them the motivation to continue and reinforces their belief in the value of their work. Thus, I must not overlook any reader who supported me with their kind and encouraging words. To each and every one of them, I extend my gratitude and the blessings from God.

# Table of Contents

# Introduction

We typically spend about twenty years in formal education, from primary school to college. Have you ever asked yourself what you remember from these long school years? Except for basic math and some fragmented knowledge, it seems we don't recall much. Oblivious people, like myself, forget almost everything.

So, why do we spend a quarter of our lives in schools and universities, one may legitimately ask? Wouldn't it be wiser to learn the fundamentals and avoid those long and tedious years of schooling? We are going to forget what we learn anyway.

I might argue that what we forget is mere information, such as "what is the capital of Norway?" However, the techniques and hacks we learned remain memorable. We may forget the raw information, but not the thinking methods behind them.

I remember a schoolmate who had insight. He once told me that when there is a question with five answers, such as "What are the five reasons for the French Revolution?" The first three answers may come to you intuitively, while the fourth may be tough to deduce, and the fifth will be impossible to obtain on your own. He was talking about patterns.

There isn't a universally agreed-upon definition of intelligence, yet I can argue that patterns are the core of intellectual thinking. I dare to define intelligence as "our capacity to see patterns." While the universe appears diverse and chaotic at first glance, deeper examination reveals resemblances: trees are similar, waterfalls fall similarly, and mountains, while rough, are also similar. Our behaviors, aspirations, and dreams all follow the same patterns. The world is not a disorganized chaos; rather, it is a cohesive whole. The uniformity lies beneath what appears to be randomness.

The naive mind is the one that walks the path of the messy world, thinks of the universe as infinite and unrelated entities, and takes each problem independently. On the contrary, the intelligent mind is the one that realizes similarity, picks up resemblance from differences, and recognizes patterns.

The second crucial criterion of human intelligence is our ability to think about ourselves and to "think about our own thinking".

Assume a rabbit was attacked by a wild dog and got paralyzed by fear. Fortunately, the dog went away without harming it. The rabbit thought, "I was supposed to run, not remain there like that. I must have been frozen with fear; what a stupid rabbit I was." If such a rabbit exists, capable of thinking about its own thoughts, it may be eligible for a college degree.

According to this definition, the majority of animals do not question their actions. They do not say to themselves, "What was I thinking?" One of the best tests in this regard is the "mirror test," a well-known test used to measure the intelligence of animals. In this test, a mirror is held in front of the animal, and researchers watch to see how it responds. Animals with low intelligence treat the mirror reflection as another member of their species and respond accordingly. However, some smart animals recognize themselves when they look in a mirror and adjust their posture to see how they appear. The dolphin is one such mammal that exhibits this behavior. It acts as if it is saying, "Well, it seems I can surf on the water, but can I balance on my tail? Why shouldn't

I try and see what would happen in the mirror?" Dolphins are undoubtedly intelligent animals.

According to the previous concept, we are considered more intelligent and wiser the more we reflect on our own thoughts and emotions.

The third criterion of intelligence is "metaphorical thinking." Typically, patterns only show up within a specific domain, such as patterns in social science or patterns in physics. However when we think metaphorically, we find that patterns are cross-disciplinary; a law of physics with the right abstraction can be found in biology or even economics.

Metaphorical thinking is the strongest faculty of the human mind. Through metaphors, everything is connected; a poem's rhythm could be compared to a mountainous terrain, a literary novel could resemble a natural landscape, and physics theories can be applied to psychology, art, or cooking. There are no borders between knowledge fields.

Whether you are an entrepreneur, researcher, employee, student, or mother at home, you have to deal with problems. However, it is unreasonable to get stuck with a problem whose solution was discovered a century ago. The fact is, it is so rare to encounter an entirely new problem pattern that has never appeared in history.

To recap: (1) think in patterns because that is how the universe is structured. (2) use metaphors because patterns are cross-disciplinary, (3) finally, think about your own thinking because this is one of the deepest characteristics of humanity.

In this book, we aim to present a simplified guide to enhance thinking for readers of all backgrounds and disciplines. We will explore the most crucial thinking strategies, emphasizing pattern recognition, metaphorical thinking, and self-awareness. By understanding and employing these tactics in various real-life situations, we can unlock the true potential of our intelligence and become more adept at problem-solving.

# Trojan horse Pattern

To win, you have to keep up with the system

# Trojan horse Pattern

You must have heard of the "Trojan horse" story in one way or another. Due to the broad popularity of the story, we have chosen it to be the first technique of thinking discussed in our book.

In ancient times, approximately around 1200 B.C., a war arose between the Romans and the inhabitants of Troy - whose remnants are located in Anatolia, Turkey. During the war, the Romans besieged the city of Troy for a prolonged period of ten years, yet they failed to conquer it. Troy's defenses were formidable, with high walls that appeared impenetrable from all sides. In this context, the story describes the ingenious concept put forth by a Roman knight known as Odysseus. His idea entailed building a huge wooden horse, concealing several knights within its hollow belly, while the Roman army and their ships pretend to depart from the vicinity.

Indeed, the idea of Odysseus was implemented, and the Trojans from atop their city walls saw the Roman ships sailing away, while the soldiers who were besieging the city withdrew. Consequently, the Trojans presumed that the Romans had finally get tired of the long siege in vain and were defeated by the hardness of their fortress. Filled with this belief, the Trojans opened the gates of the city and discovered remnants of the Roman army, including their abandoned tents, weapons, equipment, and other huge wooden horse. The Trojans deemed them as spoils and hauled them within the confines of their city walls.

At night, under the cover of darkness, the concealed 30 soldiers within the wooden horse infiltrated the city. They attacked the Trojan guards of the gate, unlocking the fort's gates from within and granting entry to the remaining Roman army, who had returned from the sea. Troy fell to the Romans during that day, leaving it razed to the ground. This momentous historical defeat was preserved by Roman poets in their epic poems, "The Iliad and The Odyssey." The tale endures, showcasing the Romans' intelligence and supremacy during that era while also offering a genuine, reusable solution for analogous situations, serving as one of the most successful patterns of unconventional thinking.

The strategic Trojan horse tactic addresses the challenge of infiltrating a city fortified by an impenetrable stronghold. The Romans' approach involved harmonizing with the prevailing system. The key to resolving this dilemma lies in posing the right question: What can effortlessly gain entry into the fortified city? The obvious answer is "the spoils", since we are at war and the spoils are the sole entity capable of entering the city under these circumstances. To effectively employ this solution, we must become the spoils ourselves, breaching the system and gaining easy access to the city. Directly confronting the system would otherwise elicit resistance. The success of this tactic hinges on our ability to seamlessly integrate with the city's dynamics, exploiting its vulnerabilities from within.

The story of Troy may not be the first to discover this technique, as its intuitive nature suggests that even clever animals may employ it for escape or hunting. By adopting the laws of a system or **disguising oneself as part of it**, gaining access becomes easier. The Trojan horse tactic extends beyond physical matter, for when we confront any balanced system and seek to disrupt its equilibrium, it naturally resists, countering our attempts at change. This concept underscores the delicate interplay between adaptation and resistance.

Consider this common example from daily life: The police investigators handled a challenge involving a drug dealer operating under diplomatic cover. The cautious suspect had fortified his villa with guards and surveillance cameras. The police team devised a plan: by deliberately cutting off power to neighboring houses, they anticipated complaints from the villa's residents to the electricity provider. Seizing the opportunity, two undercover officers disguised as maintenance workers would install surveillance devices to gather evidence and apprehend the suspect. The residents, having requested the technicians, would not suspect the undercover cops' true identities.

The previous story highlights the importance of asking the right question as the key to finding a solution. If we ask, "How can we enter the house without arousing residents' attention?" the answer would be difficult. However, by asking, "Who can easily gain access to the house?" possibilities emerge, such as electricity maintenance workers, telephone and Internet tech-support workers, or house cleaners. Based on these answers, one can devise a solution to break in.

## In Medicine (Penicillin)

Numerous diseases caused by pathogenic bacteria. Scientists have developed two types of antibacterial medicines: one that inhibits bacterial function and another that kills it. The penicillin antibiotic, which kills bacteria, was discovered by Scottish scientist Alexander Fleming in 1928. The isolation and accurate identification of the penicillin molecule were achieved ten years later by scientists Ernest Chain and Howard Florey. In recognition of their groundbreaking work, all three scientists were awarded the Nobel Prize in Physiology and Medicine in 1945.

Bacterial cells possess a protective wall that undergoes continuous growth and reinforcement. During the final stage of wall construction, the cell utilizes two acids: alanine and glycine. Penicillin, due to its chemical similarity to alanine acid, tricks bacteria into thinking it aids in wall development. However, the penicillin molecule actually breaks the wall instead of strengthening it. In the presence of a flaw or weakness in the bacterial cell wall, external water pressure overwhelms it, resulting in the instantaneous death of the bacteria. It is important to note that penicillin has no effect on animal cells in humans and animals, as they lack a wall. Simply put, penicillin deceives bacteria by employing the Trojan horse mechanism. Just as the Romans harmonized with their surroundings to infiltrate the fortified city, penicillin employs a strategic Trojan horse mechanism, capitalizing on bacterial vulnerability to bring about their downfall from within.

## In Computing (Malwares)

In computer science, "malware," particularly the one named "Trojan Horse Malware," is used by hackers to steal sensitive information like your bank account details.

The process begins when: (1) you find a free program attached to an email or available online. (2) Once downloaded and installed, the software secretly records all keystrokes you make on the keyboard. (3) When you connect to the internet, the software sends all the things you have typed to the remote hacker, including your banking credentials.

You have been robbed, yet you were part of the robbery by voluntarily downloading that program. Fraudsters and hackers deceive people using "social engineering." The free software resembles the deceptive "Trojan horse," while the recording code within it represents the hidden soldiers infiltrating at night to steal your password. Your computer is typically immune, but by allowing the thief to enter, they open the door from the inside, granting access to external criminals.

## In Other Fields

The Trojan horse thinking technique finds its application in various fields, showcasing its versatility and effectiveness. In psychology, it can be employed through cognitive strategies that exploit biases and heuristics to influence decision-making. In the realm of economics, the Trojan horse technique can be observed in marketing strategies, where businesses camouflage their advertisements as helpful or entertaining content to engage and sway consumers. In the medical field, targeted drug delivery utilizes the Trojan horse concept, with nanoparticles disguising themselves as harmless substances to selectively transport medications to specific sites in the body. In warfare, military tactics often employ decoy operations and diversionary attacks, reminiscent of the Trojan horse strategy, to deceive and overcome the enemy. Education benefits from the Trojan horse approach through innovative teaching methods that make learning engaging and enjoyable, effectively infiltrating knowledge and skills into students' minds. Furthermore, the Trojan horse thinking technique finds application in various other fields, such as cyber-security, negotiation, diplomacy, and problem-solving, enabling individuals to navigate complex systems and achieve their objectives through clever deception and strategic thinking.

## When to Employ This Thinking Tactic

This thinking pattern proves valuable when faced with an immune system that requires overcoming. It is important to note that the system doesn't necessarily need to be a physical fortress or a protected area; it can be any entity that responds with defensive pushback when challenged. Further exploration of the metaphorical use of the Trojan horse pattern will be discussed in the "Metaphor Thinking" chapter.

## Summary

The Trojan horse thinking tactic offers valuable insights for navigating and influencing various systems. It emphasizes the importance of indirect approaches to avoid immediate resistance or counter-reactions. Instead of confronting a stable system head-on, the tactic suggests leveraging the system's own dynamics and properties to achieve desired outcomes effectively.

1. This thinking technique is used to influence a system indirectly to avoid any counter-reaction.

2. Confronting any stable system directly results in a resistive reaction that reduces or prevents any changes we try to impose.

3. If you want to win, you have to go along with the system. The key to this is to ask the right question, such as, "What can naturally enter the system without resistance?"

4. You may take advantage of the system's reactions and properties to attain your own objectives.

5. Once you know the entity that can flawlessly breach the system, try to "disguise" yourself as that entity so you can overcome the system from within.

# Google Pattern

The solution you seek may have already been discovered.

# Google Pattern

The story of the invention of the search engine "Google" is one of those truly captivating stories. This company has become one of the most important and largest companies in modern history, and it controls the organization of information around the globe, so to speak. There may not be anyone on this planet today who does not know Google or has never heard of it. That is why Randall Strauss titled his book about Google "Planet Google". Google's revenues were only $400 million at the end of 2000. Alphabet Inc. reported its revenue for the second quarter of 2021 at $61.9 billion, catching up with Apple and Microsoft as the third corporation to reach a market value of one trillion dollars.

We may wonder: what is the reason behind this astonishing success? Is it the company's excellent management? The intelligent engineers they hire? Or perhaps the large capital that has contributed to this remarkable growth? But could it be simpler than that? In reality, Google had a mere new "idea" to solve a problem, and that idea turned out to be like the hen that lays golden eggs. Google leveraged this creative idea at an opportune moment in history. In other words, Google possessed a novel and unique "thinking tactic" to address a significant challenge of our time.

## What is the Google Pattern?

Prior to delving into the story, it is crucial to emphasize that the Google pattern has nothing to do with computer science. The approach employed by Google does not necessitate any prior knowledge of programming or mathematics. In fact, the core of the concept has nothing to do with technology at all.

The tale unfolds with two students, namely "Larry Page" and "Sergey Brin," who were admitted to Stanford University in the United States in 1996 to pursue doctoral studies and research. Interestingly, despite being relative strangers at the time, they found themselves involved in numerous disagreements upon their initial encounter. Petty arguments seemed to arise out of nowhere, leading each to hold a disdainful view of the other. However, over time, this discord transformed into a deep and enduring friendship that will continue for many years.

Both Larry and Sergey possessed exceptional intellects and bright minds. While Larry Page was keen on problem-solving, Sergey Brin showcased remarkable programming skills. Fortunately, they mutually agreed to collaborate on a doctoral project about enabling people to search the Internet effectively, eventually giving rise to the famous search engine known as "Google". Meanwhile, the Internet was undergoing rapid spreading and expansion, with individuals relying on "directories" or "search engines" such as Yahoo, Lycos, and AltaVista to access information online. During that era, Yahoo held the status of being the most popular choice among users.

The Internet was like a vast book with several million pages at that time, and the search engines functioned as the index of this book. Browsing a book with millions of pages manually is not an easy task; it is difficult to find relevant information, and you must use a kind of index. This necessity led to the emergence of internet-search companies such as Yahoo and many others.

There were two primary types of internet search companies at that time. The first type was called "Directory," which classified the Internet into main and sub-topics such as education, health, agriculture, politics, and so on. The user clicks on the main topic "education" and navigates its sub-topics, such as primary education, secondary education, and higher education. Selecting primary education would further narrow down the options, showing a list of primary schools, for example. By following this hierarchical structure, users could explore the Internet until they found the desired website. The second type of internet search company was called "Search Engine," which differs from "Directory" in that it allowed users to directly search for topics by typing keywords into an empty search box, similar to Google. For instance, typing "children's education" would generate a list of results containing relevant school websites. The search engine approach provided a more direct and immediate way to find information compared to the hierarchical navigation offered by directories.

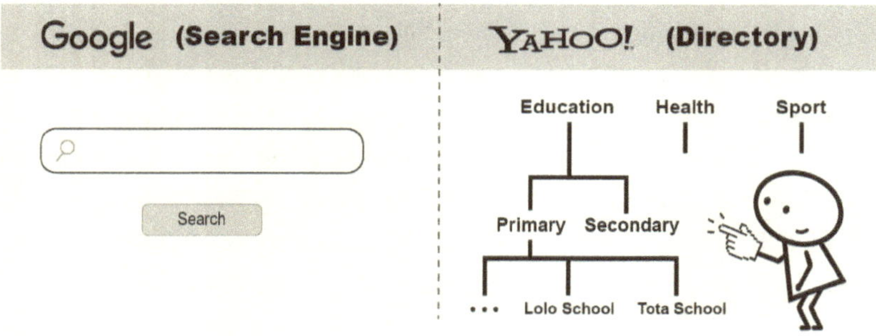


As the internet expanded and the number of websites reached almost 2 billion, the task of searching became increasingly challenging. When you are searching for a specific topic like "primary education," the search results would often yield hundreds of pages related to children's education. However, how can we determine the best school from those hundreds results? The results lacked organization. It became necessary to have a more refined search mechanism that could identify the best answer and present it prominently at the top of the search results. This would enable users to find the most relevant and valuable information more efficiently.


## How Did Search Engines Work Before Google?

Imagine visiting a bookstore in search of a cookbook and seeking assistance from a five-year-old boy working as the seller. Eager to help, the young boy embarks on a rather childish approach by counting the word "cook" in each book he encounters. Naively, he believes that the book with the most numbers of the word "cook" must undoubtedly be the best one. However, the book he ultimately brings you turns out to be of poor quality. This scenario was exactly the way search engines operated before the advent of Google.

In the past, if you were to look up the word "news," for example, instead of directing you to reputable sources like "BBC" or "Al-Jazeera," the search engine might lead you to an insignificant website simply because it featured the term "news" more frequently. These outdated search engines ranked websites based on word repetition, often resulting in poor search results.

This realization prompted Larry Page to ask, "How can we enhance Internet search?" He grasped the necessity for a mechanism that could elevate significant results, ensuring that searches like "software" highlight major software companies such as Microsoft and Apple, and "cars" showcase foremost brands like Toyota or Mercedes at the list's pinnacle. Driven by this vision, Page aimed to revolutionize the search experience by developing algorithms capable of discerning relevance. His aspiration was to refine searches to a point where users effortlessly found precisely what they sought, amplifying user satisfaction and the efficiency of online information retrieval. This marked the inception of Google, a search engine that would transform the digital landscape and become the ideal user-friendly online search engine.

## How Larry Discovered A Solution for Organizing the Internet?

Larry's upbringing in an academic family played a pivotal role in his quest. Both his parents, who were college teachers with experience in scientific publications, exposed him to the world of academic journals and their ranking methods. In academic literature, when a scientific paper or book is frequently mentioned or "cited" by other papers, it indicates its importance. For instance, renowned scientists like "Isaac Newton" and "Einstein" have been cited in thousands of other publications, underscoring their significance. Recognizing this technique, Larry wondered whether it could be applied to address the challenge of ranking internet pages.

The solution to the internet ranking problem had already been present for many years within the domain of "academic publications." However, it had gone unnoticed until Larry's insightful observation.

## How are Scientific Publications Ranked?

Long before the advent of the internet, universities worldwide used a system to organize scientific research publications. Consider this scenario: Suppose you made a groundbreaking discovery like—a cure for cancer—and published a scholarly paper showing your findings. As news of your amazing breakthrough spread globally, other students engaged in cancer research worldwide cited your work and referenced you in their own papers. The significance of your research grew with each citation and mention by these researchers. If the number of researchers citing your work were to reach, say, one million, it would place your research as the most important cancer research globally. This interconnected web of citations solidified the collaborative nature of scientific progress, where each brick in the edifice of knowledge is laid upon the foundations of those who came before.

## Applying the Pattern to the Internet

Unlike scientific papers, internet pages lack explicit citations. However, Larry and Sergey noticed something on the internet that is quite similar to the citation: "the links". All internet pages contain hyperlinks to other websites. Leveraging this observation, Google devised an equation to calculate the number of links pointing to a specific website:

$$(x)^{\cdot} = \sum_{k=0}^{n} \binom{n}{k} x^k a^{n-k}$$

For example, the above equation calculates the number of websites that are linked to the BBC Website. And also the number of websites that linked to the CNN website. By comparing the two numbers of links, the website with the highest number will receive a higher ranking. For instance, if the BBC has 900 websites linked to it and CNN has 700, the BBC will come up first when someone searches for the word "news".

Back-links serve a function comparable to citations in academic journals. When a website offers valuable content, others often reference and link back to it. Numerous newspaper and television channel websites derive news from the BBC and attribute it as their source, thereby including a link back to the BBC. While comprehending the intricacies of Google's mathematical equation may not be necessary, grasping the underlying thinking pattern holds significance. Using this citation-like method, Google automatically organized all internet websites into a hierarchical order based on their significance. Nowadays, if you conduct a search by typing the word "news," the most reputable news websites will prominently appear at the top of the search results.

## Summary of What Google Does

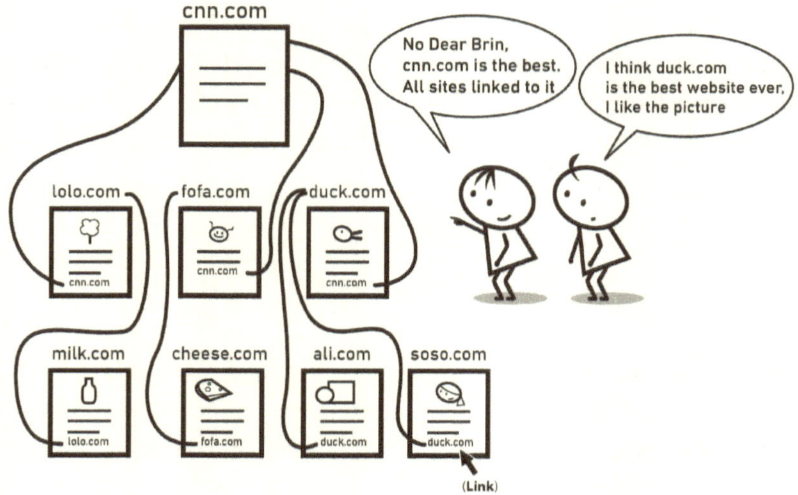


There are eight websites displayed in the image above. How can we order them in terms of importance?

According to Google's method, the website (cnn.com) is the most important because three websites refer back to it. Following that, the website (duck.com) ranks second because two sites refer back to it. The websites (lolo.com) and (fofa.com) share the third-place position since they each receive references from one site, indicating equal importance. The other four websites are ranked relatively low.

The profound lesson learned from the Google thinking technique is not about how to arrange things; it emphasizes the crucial message that "solutions can be derived from another field". In essence, one can uncover that the problem they are currently struggling with might have already been resolved in an entirely different discipline. For instance, a management dilemma may have been effectively tackled years ago in engineering or even in the realm of art. Larry Page and Sergey Brin exemplify this notion by discovering the solution to the "Internet ranking" predicament within the realm of "academic publications."

## Cross-disciplinary Solutions

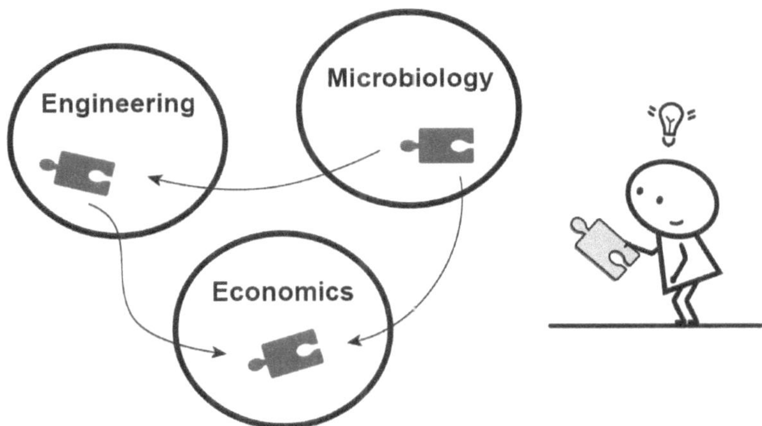


Throughout history, numerous strategies and famous solutions have been borrowed from one domain to another, leading to remarkable advancements in various fields. The process of cross-disciplinary borrowing has sparked innovation and breakthroughs. For instance, the concept of "divide and conquer" strategy, widely used in military tactics, has found applications in computer science algorithms. The field of economics has borrowed concepts like supply and demand from physics to understand market dynamics. In medicine, the idea of vaccination draws upon principles of immunology and the concept of herd immunity from epidemiology. The design of wind turbines used in renewable energy generation has been inspired by the aerodynamics of airplane wings. The invention of the Gutenberg printing press revolutionized communication and drew upon the wine press technology. The study of fractal geometry, initially developed in mathematics, has been applied to computer graphics, art, and architecture. These examples demonstrate the power of interdisciplinary borrowing, where ideas, strategies, and solutions from one domain can be successfully translated and leveraged in completely different fields, fostering progress and opening new avenues of exploration.

## Summary

1. Solutions can be borrowed and applied from one scientific domain to another, enabling cross-disciplinary innovation.

2. Problem-solving doesn't necessarily require expertise in the respective field. By simplifying problems, individuals from diverse backgrounds can recognize similarities with analogous solved problems. For instance, Google's ranking mechanism could have been discovered by a librarian or a teacher.

3. The relative importance of things is often determined by external factors rather than their intrinsic value. People's reviews, internet backlinks, and citations are examples of such external factors.

4. Embracing a multidisciplinary approach can lead to breakthrough solutions. By combining insights and methodologies from different fields, new perspectives and inventions can be revealed.

34

# Outside the Box Pattern

The answer lies behind the unreasonable question

# Outside the Box Pattern

We frequently encounter the phrase "thinking outside the box," but how can we do such a thing? Is there a specific method to thinking outside the box, or is it a mere coincidence that we can't control and deliberately make or engage in?

In this story, which occurred around the year 2009, professor "Tina Seliq" at Stanford University, USA, was conducting a test for students as part of the program "Stanford Technology Ventures". She divided the students into 14 teams and gave each team a sealed envelope containing five dollars. Each team was asked to invest this money in the best feasible way within just two hours. The team may plan for two or three days, but once the envelope is opened, the team has only two hours to implement their investment plan. On the final day of the test, each team is required to provide a brief explanation of what they have done within a three-minute timeframe and present their project to the rest of the class.

Some of the obvious ideas that were offered at the time were to sell lemonade and provide car wash services; the team purchases simple materials with their five dollars and provides the service for a period of two hours to earn some money. However, resourceful students from Stanford University managed to surpass expectations with their unconventional approaches.

One of the winning teams did the following: they realized that the city was full of long lines in front of restaurants, especially on Saturdays. So they positioned team members at various restaurants to hold spots in line and then sold those coveted positions to eager customers. Remarkably, this team utilized the full five-day timeframe provided rather than restricting themselves to the two-hour limit.

Another winning team had a clever idea as well. They created a platform to give free "bikes tire pressure measuring" services on the university campus. If the tires need to be filled, they charge one dollar. After one hour of their trial period, the team began to accept donations instead of the fixed price, and the results were even better. The "Restaurant Project" and the "Bicycles Project" each brought in several hundred dollars and were admired by the professor.

The top-winning project, which yielded an impressive $650 in revenue, was conceived by a team that approached things from a unique perspective. Recognizing an overlooked asset among their peers, this team realized that their most valuable resource was not the five dollars or the two-hour timeframe, but rather the "three-minute presentation slot" on the final day. While others failed to perceive the presentation time as a valuable resource, this team went to sell the time slot to a corporation seeking to advertise to students. They showcased the advertisement for three minutes during the class and earned $650, all while their original five-dollar envelope remained sealed. This approach is turning insignificant resources into lucrative opportunities.

The story serves as a beautiful illustration of thinking outside the box. The term "box" symbolizes the intellectual framework that confines and limits our thinking. In this case, all the students were fixated on the five-dollar envelope. They were trapped in it. Fairly, it is natural for them to solely consider the five dollars and overlook other possibilities, especially since the professor taught them it their only capital. By challenging this conventional thinking, the winning team break free from common-sense mental limits.

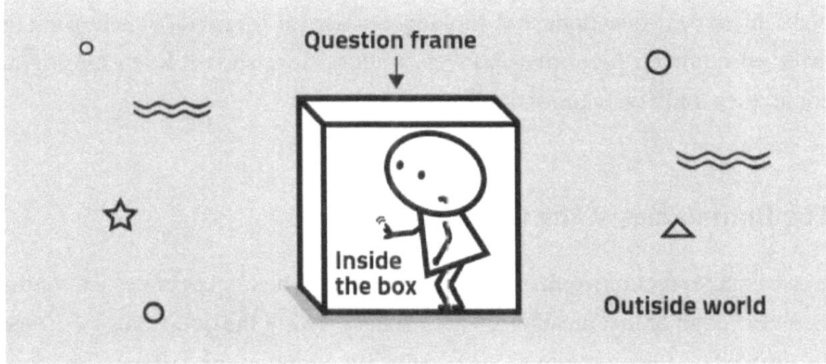


The winning team had the courage to ask, "What resources do we possess beyond the five dollars?" It was at this point that they were able to escape from their mental captivity, giving rise to new possibilities. They directed their attention towards something that wasn't a traditional resource at all—rather, it resided on the opposite side of the spectrum: "the evaluation process". This is akin to facing a challenging exam and reading all the available books, only to realize that the solutions were hidden within the very questions of the exam itself. Their shift in perspective highlights the transformative power of lateral thinking, emphasizing that breakthroughs often emerge when we redefine the boundaries of our problem-solving landscape and rediscover unseen resources.

## A General Rule for Thinking Outside the Box

The Stanford experiment showed that the human mind is capable of thinking outside the box if we stimulate it with the right question, such as "Are there any hidden resources beyond the five dollars?" On the other hand, embracing negative claims like "We mustn't consider anything beyond the five dollars" blocks our creativity. The mind should be liberated from restrictions, no matter how strong they are. It is not a simple task, but it is the only way to access any hidden chances. In a nutshell, the key to unlocking creativity lies in daring to pose questions that defy logic or appear irrational. It is beyond the realm of common logic that innovative ideas flourish, while within logical boundaries, only conventional ideas reside.

## The Boundaries of the Question

It is crucial to recognize that thinking outside the box necessitates examining the very "edge of the question". This means viewing the question as if it were the answer or a resource in its own right. By adopting this perspective, fresh insights emerge.

The following is a hypothetical conversation between two individuals where the second person finds themselves mentally trapped within the box:

**Person 1:** Is it feasible to achieve victory without opening the envelope or using the five dollars?

**Person 2:** That's not possible. The professor told us that this is our capital, so we must use it.

**Person 1:** How can we generate a thousand dollars in profit within two hours?

**Person 2:**    Well, it's impossible. With just five dollars, we should focus on a reasonable profit.

**Person 1:**    What other resources do we have to invest in apart from the five dollars and the two-hour timeframe?

**Person 2:**    We don't have anything else. Let's not overthink it and solely rely on what we have.

Each time Person 2 expresses "I can't" or "it is impossible," the problem becomes unsolvable for them. Instead of using such terms, train yourself to rephrase the questions as follows: "Let's assume it's possible to earn a thousand dollars. How can we accomplish this earning?" By reframing the perspective, we open the door for ingenious possibilities.

## Example

In the given drawing, there is a plot of land that needs to be evenly distributed among four brothers while maintaining the same shape. Take a moment to attempt to solve the problem before proceeding to read the answer.

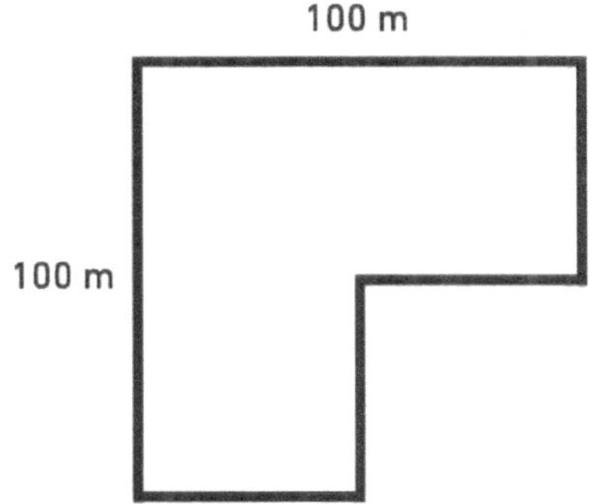

## The Solution

You can arrive at the solution through various trials. One approach involves completing the outer square and then drawing another small square inside, which reveals the shape in grey—an appropriate answer to the question.

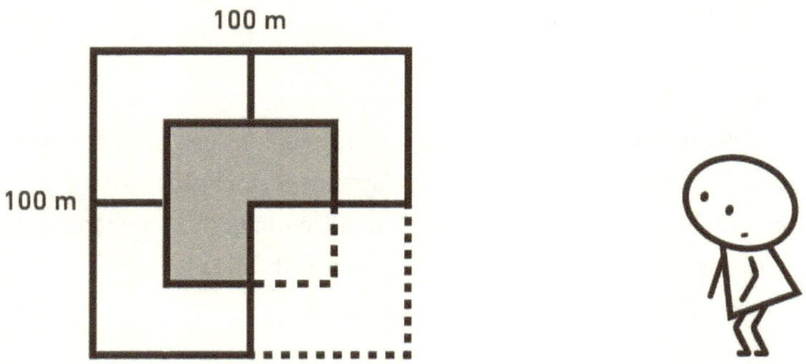


However, the easiest and most straightforward method is to consider, "What if the question's shape itself is the answer?" When you contemplate this, you'll quickly realize that the shape of the provided land itself represents the answer when minimized. This is a simple illustration of thinking "outside the box".

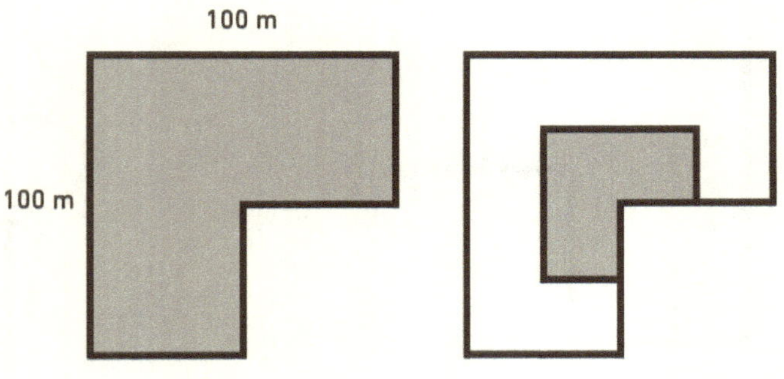

## Advanced Example 2

In times of war, military intelligence must safeguard critical information from the enemy's prying eyes, as its revelation could alter the course of the conflict. Concealing communications becomes a paramount concern for the military.

One of the ancient methods of concealing information, employed by the Romans, involved shaving a soldier's head, tattooing a message on the scalp, and allowing the hair to regrow. The soldier would then deliver the message, leaving the enemy oblivious to its presence hidden beneath the hair.

Throughout history, techniques for concealing vital messages have evolved. Steganography, the art of concealing data in photographs, provides a modern-day approach. For instance, a covert spy can encode a message within a seemingly innocent photograph, like a wedding or holiday snapshot, and transmit it via email. Even if authorities monitored the spy's activities, they would only discover ordinary images in the emails.

Hiding a message in an ordinary image involves exploiting the fact that computer data is stored as numbers. By replacing some of the image's numerical values with others representing letters, the spy can conceal the message. Although this process causes minimal distortion in the image, it remains imperceptible to the naked eye.

Consider the following scenario: our covert spy discovers an air base in the desert and intends to alert their country's intelligence by sending a one-word message (DESERT). To begin, the spy must assign a specific number to each letter of the alphabet, converting the message into numerical form. For instance, "D" would be represented as "15". Additionally, the spy must hide the message letters in predetermined positions, allowing the recipient to extract the hidden letters. Without knowledge of these hiding spots and the method used, the recipient would be unable to unveil the concealed message.

The spy and their counterpart in the homeland should have prearranged the locations for hiding letters.

Now, you have a basic understanding of steganography, the science and art of concealing messages. However, it is essential to note that hiding text in an image induces some image distortion. With the advancements in detection methods, there is a risk that authorities might detect slight distortions and suspect something hidden within the image. Although they might not be able to decipher the message, mere suspicion could jeopardize the covert spy's life.

## The Question:

You have been tasked by the intelligence service to enhance the method of communicating secret information within photos. The goal is to reduce image distortion caused by text insertion and safeguard the covert spy from detection. Using "outside the box" thinking, attempt to devise a way to conceal a message within an image with minimal distortion.

The figure shows that digital images are made up of numerical values

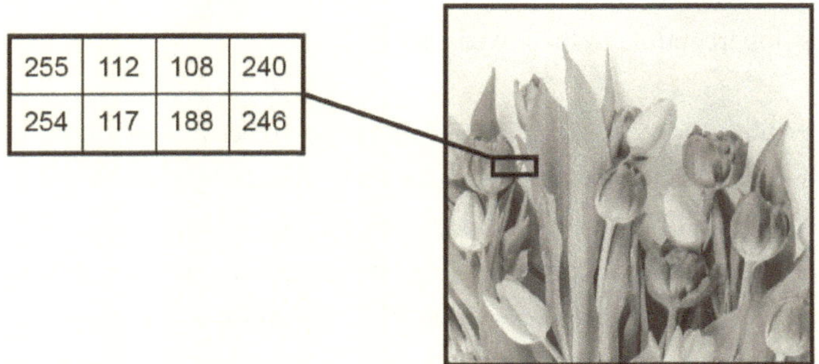

## The Solution:

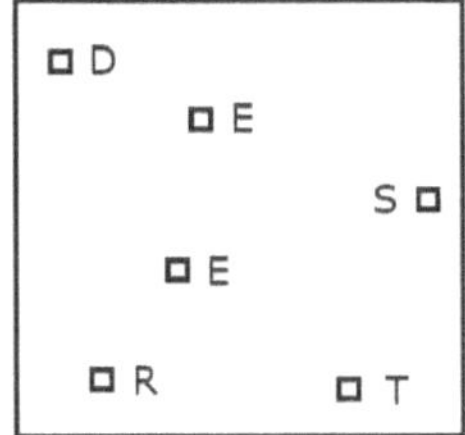


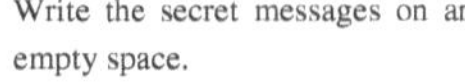

Write the secret messages on an empty space.

Search many images until you find the exact letters' values

Map each image's correct pixel with the required letter.

When aiming to think outside the box, dare to push the boundaries beyond what is conventionally deemed possible.

Recognize that any attempt to input text by altering image pixels will inevitably cause image distortion. It is simply impossible to insert values without changing the image. Embrace this seemingly impossible challenge and ask yourself, "How can we insert text into an image without altering it?" By refraining from self-limiting beliefs and giving it thought, a possible solution emerges.

Instead of changing the image's pixels, we can start with a blank white area and fixate the message letters in some known positions. Next, load multiple images instead of one and search their pixels for values corresponding to the letters. Map one suitable image for each letter, creating an image mosaic containing the secret message. Indeed, you may crop any unnecessary image frames.

In this manner, if authorities intercept the collage image, they will have no way of determining whether it conceals a secret message or not. Each image remains untouched, free from any changes or distortions. We have compensated for the process of "modifying one image" by using "several images that are completely unmodified". Achieving this solution hinges on asking the seemingly impossible question of how to attain zero distortion.

45

## Summary

Embrace daring questions and never be bound by what is reasonable or possible. If asked to achieve a profit of hundreds, why not consider aiming for a million?

1. Unreasonable questions won't cause the universe to collapse. Explore the unknown and challenge the norm.

2. Avoid declaring "that can't be done," because only then will it become impossible for your mind.

3. Seek answers in unconventional places, including the question itself; sometimes the answer is somehow concealed within the question's frame.

4. Embrace extremes like zero and infinity. People often dismiss them as unattainable; however, thinking about the impossible is what leads to achieving impossible results.

# The Goat Pattern

In confusing probability problems, eliminate time.

# The Goat Pattern

The story goes that the American journalist and writer, Marilyn Vos Savant, had a column called "Ask Marilyn" in "Parade" magazine, where readers could send their questions and she would answer them. In 1990, Marilyn received a question from a reader named Craig F. Whitaker regarding a TV contest show scenario.

The reader's question was about a TV contest show with three closed doors. Behind one of the doors was a car, and behind the other two were goats. The participant had to randomly select one of the doors to win the car as a prize. After making their choice, the TV program host would then open another door, not the one the participant picked. revealing a goat. The reader asked whether the participant should stick with their initial choice or switch to the other unopened door.

So, should the participant keep their first door or switch to the other one?

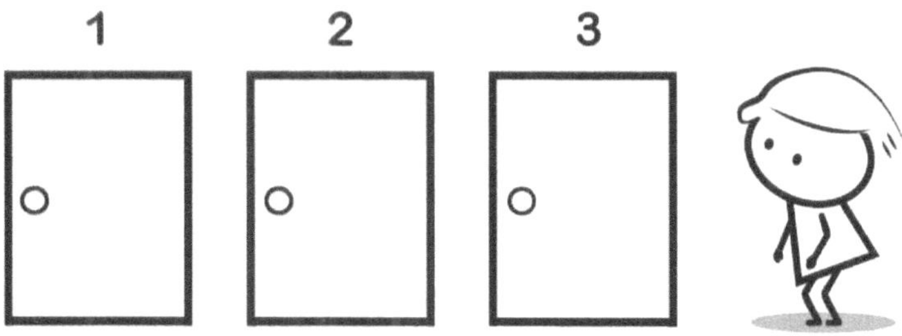

## The Solution

At first glance, the question might seem meaningless. With two doors left—one concealing the car and the other the goat—it could be assumed that each door holds a 50 percent chance. Consequently, changing the door might seem pointless. However, Marilyn, the journalist, offered a different perspective, asserting that "It is better to change the door."

The solution to this question lies in switching to the unopened door. This counterintuitive outcome hinges on probability. Initially, the participant faces a 1/3 chance of selecting the car-containing door and a 2/3 chance of picking a goat. Even after the host reveals a goat door, the probabilities associated with the participant's initial choice remain unchanged. Nevertheless, the unopened door now carries the remaining 2/3 probability of concealing the car behind it.

Despite this logical explanation, many individuals still struggle to accept the idea that changing the door is the optimal strategy in this puzzle.

## Who is Marilyn?

Marilyn is no ordinary journalist; she, in fact, secured the record for the highest IQ ever recorded in the Guinness Book of Records—a distinction that persisted until the encyclopedia removed the IQ category in 1990. At the young age of 10, Marilyn took an IQ test and achieved a remarkable score of 228. To provide context, a standard individual's IQ typically falls within the range of 90-110, while anything surpassing 120 is deemed intelligent, and figures exceeding 140 are labeled as genius.

This riddle has sparked psychological studies, driven by a quest to fathom why the majority of people steadfastly maintain that the odds remain equal, negating any necessity to change doors. The riddle unfurls within a scenario wherein a participant should invariably switch doors after the host reveals a goat behind one of the alternative doors. This strategic switch enhances the participant's likelihood of winning a car.

Intriguingly, the riddle transformed into a topic of public discourse, triggering debates and controversies across diverse American institutions. This included esteemed scientific bodies like NASA, public institutions, and colleges, all finding themselves embroiled in discussions about the puzzle.

## Further Explanation

Marilyn's solution to the riddle is indeed correct: to increase your odds of winning the car, you should change the door. Despite this, many people are not convinced of its validity. Some skeptics conducted an actual experiment on the riddle to measure the odds between those who change the door and those who stick with their initial choice. The results were clear: those who change the door have a "two-thirds" probability of winning, while those who stick with their first choice only have a "third" probability of winning. This counterintuitive outcome challenges our instinctive notions about probability and decision-making.

When Marilyn published her answer in the magazine column, it sparked significant disagreement from readers. The magazine received around 10,000 letters from angry readers, including about a thousand from Ph.D. holders, all claiming that Marilyn's answer was wrong. Many of these letters came from prestigious universities and were written by mathematics departments and upset professors criticizing Marilyn's response. Despite the backlash, Marilyn stood her ground and remained firm in her answer.

It is important to note that the TV show host, who reveals the doors, will always try to keep you from winning. Thus, the host will always make sure to open a door with a goat behind it. If you choose the first door and it has a goat behind it, the host will reveal the second door with a goat. As a result, the car will be behind the third door that you did not initially select, giving this situation a "two-thirds" chance of occurring.

On the other hand, if you initially choose the door with the car, the host will still choose a door with a goat and open it. In this case, the possibility of this happening is only "one third." Therefore, the first situation (where you choose the door with a goat) is the most likely to occur, and you should bet on it and change the door.

Marilyn simplifies this matter with the following analogy: "Imagine that there are a hundred doors, behind all of them are goats, except for one door with a car behind it. If you choose one of these doors, let's say door number one, then the host opens all other doors except door number 79. Wouldn't you change to choose this door?" The logic here is the same as in the original riddle scenario, where changing the door increases your chances of winning the car.

This clever comparison highlights the underlying principle that altering your choice maximizes your potential outcome.

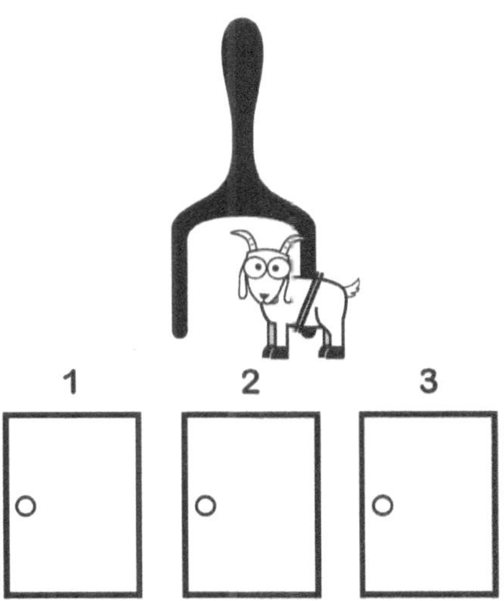

You can adopt your own unique way of comprehending the Monty Hall problem. I developed an approach called the "fork" method. Imagine you have a fork with two teeth—one tooth represents your initial door choice, while the other tooth is invariably linked to a goat (the host will always reveal a goat). The probability of you picking the first goat and the other fork tooth leading to the second goat, or vice versa, always stands at two-thirds. Hence, this scenario becomes the most likely event, making it clear that changing the door is the better strategy. The fork is "swapping" the likelihood literally.

You should notice that the fork is time-transcendent in that it picks the goat at the very moment you pick a door. If you found this riddle challenging to understand, don't feel discouraged about your intelligence. Rest assured, it puzzled numerous intelligent individuals. Even Nobel Prize physicists consistently provided the wrong answer and staunchly defended it, exemplifying the difficulty of overcoming intuitive biases. Cognitive psychologist Massimo Piattelli points out that no other statistical puzzle comes as close to consistently confounding everyone as this riddle.

Surprisingly, a study revealed that pigeons, when repeatedly exposed to the problem, quickly learned to always switch doors, unlike humans, who often struggle to do so. This highlights the innate difficulty humans face in overcoming their intuitive biases.

Asha Volokh (2015) underlines the flaw in any explanation that rigidly claims the probability of door one being 1/3 and unchangeable. Probabilities represent our ignorance about the world, and with new information, the extent of our ignorance can change. Therefore, it is crucial to consider the logic behind the correct solution rather than being bound by intuitive assumptions. Embracing the statistically superior strategy of changing doors is essential to optimizing your chances of winning the coveted prize in the Monty Hall problem."

Interestingly, if the host also has no knowledge of what is behind the doors, and they randomly choose a door with a goat. In this scenario, the probability remains equal (50%) for both - keeping the door and changing it. The host's ignorance does not influence the outcome, and the puzzle's probabilities remain unchanged.

## The Thinking Pattern Underlying the Monty Hall Puzzle

The key to understanding problems with two or more perplexingly connected actions is to eliminate time completely and think regardless of their past-future setup. By considering the events as if they occur mechanically and concurrently, one can better grasp the overall structure of the problem and find a clearer solution.

## Summary

To understand problems with perplexing connected actions, eliminate the time dimension, consider the events as if they occur mechanically and concurrently for a clearer mental image.

1. Eliminate time to see the panoramic picture of present-past-future.

2. Employ a conceptual mechanical linkage between any associated actions, like the "fork" example. To aid visualization.

3. The solution should reveal itself through (1) and (2).

4. Critical thinking is essential in probability problems; intuition may not always be accurate.

5. Probabilities arise from a lack of information; new information can alter the odds.

6. In probability problems, future events may be influenced by the past.

54

## Human-Related Pattern

# Belief Pattern

To change someone's behavior, make them believe

# Belief Pattern

In January 2004, a woman in Grand Rapids, USA, was involved in an accident when she crossed a red light and collided with another car at the intersection. The unusual aspect of the incident was that she hit the third or fourth car that had passed in front of her after a considerable delay since the light had turned red. The investigation revealed that the woman was traveling at 77 kilometers per hour without using her brakes at all at the time of the collision. Tragically, a twelve-year-old child lost their life in this accident.

Witnesses who saw the accident informed the investigators that the driver was not looking down, so it was ruled out that she was texting, which is a common cause of such accidents. Instead, she was looking straight through the windshield and appeared to be focused on driving through the intersection. However, she failed to notice two cars passing in front of her before colliding with the third vehicle.

Researchers attributed this phenomenon to "Inattention Blindness Caused by Cognitive Distraction." It was later discovered that the woman was talking on her phone, which affected her ability to perceive the red traffic light correctly. Remarkably, she wasn't holding the phone in her hand but was using the car's hands-free microphone.

Studies reveal that drivers talking on the phone while driving, regardless of holding it or using the car's microphone, "look at" objects without truly "seeing" them. These distracted drivers miss about 50% of their surroundings due to cognitive distractions from phone conversations, leading to potential hazards on the road.

The woman responsible for the previous accident faced a conviction of negligent homicide, altering her life and that of the deceased child's family forever. Similar accidents occur globally every day, arising from our profound ignorance of the brain and its functions.

People often believe planes are safer than cars, yet the "American Safety Organization" indicates that the number of lives lost in road accidents yearly is equivalent to a plane with 100 passengers crashing every day for an entire year. In the US, car accidents claim over 30,000 lives annually, and worldwide, the World Health Organization estimates 1.3 million deaths from road accidents each year. The WHO also contends that "Hands-free phones are not much safer than hand-held phone sets."

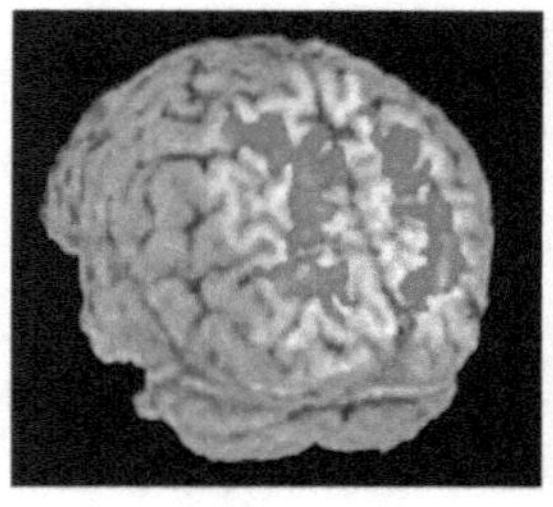 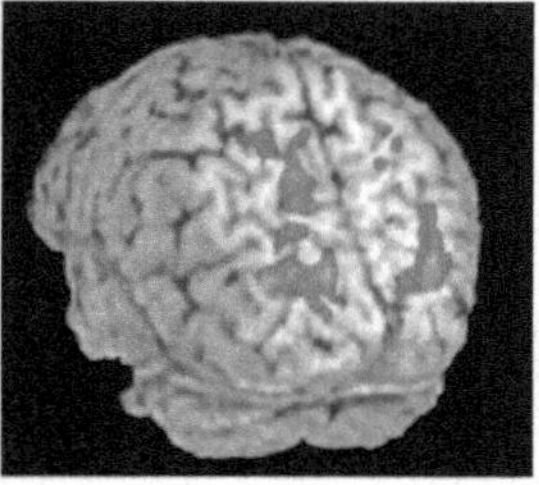 

Driving alone          Driving with sentence
                       listening

Source: Functioning Magnetic Resonance Imaging, Carnegie Mellon

Traffic laws in most countries prohibit talking on mobile phones while driving due to the hand being occupied, but this gives the misleading impression that using the car's microphone is safe. Brain activity associated with driving decreases by 37% when the driver is listening to someone speak (Carnegie Mellon University).

The mind cannot handle two tasks simultaneously, and this misunderstanding, along with car manufacturers' perceptions and laws permitting hands-free phone use, contributes to thousands of deaths annually.

## The Brain is Insane

You can think of the brain as a machine similar to a bread toaster. It cannot distinguish between a shoe and a loaf of bread. However, when you put this machine on your head, like a helmet, you begin to comprehend the world. This is where we refer to it as the "mind." The brain is often mistaken for the mind. The brain is a dumb, jelly-like substance, while the mind is the awakened experience of a lucid "you" utilizing your brain.

## The Fire Truck with Two Hoses

Imagine a fire truck equipped with dual high-pressure water hoses, both gushing water at the same time. However, you can only grip one hose at a time. As you hold onto one hose, the other twists and writhes like a snake, wildly spraying water in all directions. Similarly, attempting to drive while talking on the phone is akin to managing two hoses pumping water, but your mind can only concentrate on one at a time - either the phone call or the driving. This vivid analogy underscores the challenge of divided attention and the potential risks involved. Just as the hoses can lose control, so too can our focus on the road when distracted.

Focusing on driving enables you to handle everything effectively. You can clearly see the red traffic light and steer skillfully around obstacles. However, the Incoming calls will seem like a jumble of meaningless noise in your ear. Conversely, shifting your mental focus to the phone call turns driving into a car with literally no driver.

Consider this analogy: Have you ever poured water into your car's tank instead of fuel? Most likely not, and it's not merely because of your good morals. The reason lies in understanding and belief. Your education, experience with gasoline, and knowledge of the combustion cycle convince you that engines require fuel. This belief prevents you from ever attempting to fill the tank with water. In a similar vein, you don't try to open doors in the opposite direction or put metal in microwaves. It's not a matter of ethics, but about beliefs shaping our actions. Criminals wouldn't even pour water into their car's tank.

## The Myth of Multitasking

Cognitive scientists reveal that the human mind doesn't perform true multitasking like computers. Instead, it rapidly switches between tasks, creating an "illusion" of simultaneous processing. When driving, talking on the phone, and listening to the radio, our brain allocates milliseconds to each task in rapid succession. This creates the illusion of performing these actions concurrently, while they actually happen in sequence. Our cognition is not divisible.

Have you ever found yourself lower the radio volume after taking a wrong turn? This happens because the error demands more thought, consuming our mental capacity, leaving no room for anything else to process. So we instinctively turn off the radio. This response shows how the brain prioritize cognitive resources in moments of heightened focus.

Receiving a critical phone call can similarly occupy our thoughts entirely, leaving the brain overwhelmed. When overloaded, the brain begins to chop off sensory information and throw it away at random. The thrown scene could be a red traffic signal or a child crossing in front of you. Whatever it is, you'll never see what was cut off, even if it's right in front of your eyes.

## The Man Who Attempted Suicide

In this incident, a young man, let's call him "Dan," was suffering from depression and being treated by a doctor. His wife's abandonment deepened his depression, leading him to intend suicide. Dan ingested all of his depression pills at once, but soon, the fear of death overwhelmed him with regret. He urgently called an ambulance to confess what he had done. At the hospital, Dan's condition rapidly deteriorated, and his blood pressure dropped significantly.

The hospital doctors, aware of the seriousness of the situation, contacted Dan's treating doctor to determine the type of drug he had taken so that they could administer appropriate treatment before it was too late. To their surprise, Dan's doctor revealed that he had not prescribed any real medication. Instead, the pills he gave Dan were merely sugar pills intended to create a placebo effect, making the patient believe he was receiving treatment. Astonishingly, Dan's life was nearly claimed by mere sugar candies because of his belief that he had ingested a dangerous medicine. This phenomenon is known as the "Nocebo Effect," where one's beliefs can profoundly influence the body's response. This underscores the intricate relationship between the mind and the body, demonstrating how negative expectations can trigger genuine physical reactions with potentially fatal consequences. It highlights the importance of considering both psychological and physiological factors in healthcare.

## Water Drops Experiment

In his 1996 book "The Lost Art of Healing," American cardiologist Bernard Lawn recounts an experiment from 1936 in India. A condemned prisoner was given a choice between hanging or death by gradual blood dripping. Opting for the latter, believing it to be less painful.

On the designated day, they blindfolded the convict, tied him up, and positioned empty containers under a water tank to simulate water droplets falling into them. Simultaneously, fake scratches were made on the man's wrists to deceive him further. As the "execution" proceeded, the prisoner heard the sound of water drops, which he believed to be his own blood dripping. The intensity started fast and gradually decreased. Believing he was losing blood, the young man's heart stopped, and he died without any actual blood loss. This disturbing demonstration underscores the profound impact our thoughts can have on our physical bodies. It's a tragic reminder of the mind's power over even the most fundamental physiological processes and it also raises ethical questions about the manipulation of beliefs and its unintended consequences on human lives.

## The Mindset's Power

Our third account is a popular tale. It tells of a warship from a certain nation's naval forces conducting maneuvers at sea for training. The air was foggy, and the view was dim and unclear. Suddenly, a small civilian ship emerged in front of the battleship. Radio communication ensued:

Battleship Commander: Deviate 15 degrees north to avoid collision.

Civilian Ship Captain: I suggest changing course 15 degrees south to avoid collision.

Battleship Commander: General William Frederick commands; change your course immediately.

Ship Captain: No, it's Lieutenant David. Change your course.

Battleship Commander, angry: We are an aircraft carrier with heavy weapons. Change your direction or I'll take countermeasures for the barge's safety.

Captain - Sir, here is the lighthouse.

This narrative illustrates the consequences of misunderstanding. Due to the Commander's mistaken belief, the battleship was about to engage with the lighthouse. When we have a fixed mindset, we act upon it. The US Navy deems this story untrue, but even if fictional, it highlights the concept of the wrong mental image and its impact on our behavior.

## Exercise Experiment

In 2007, Harvard University psychologists Alia J. Crum and Ellen J. Langer carried out a study named "Mindset Matters: Exercise and the Placebo Effect." The research involved 84 female cleaners from seven different hotels. These workers were divided into two groups. The first group was informed that their room cleaning duties is providing a good exercise for the body and promoted a moderate and healthy lifestyle. The second group, however, received no such information. After a month, both groups underwent examination, and the results were noteworthy: The first group, believing they were exercising during their regular housekeeping tasks, experienced positive medical outcomes, including "weight loss, decreased blood pressure, and reduced body fat." On the other hand, the second group showed no changes in their medical results.

This phenomenon is known as the "Placebo Effect," which refers to any positive effect that arises from an individual's mindset rather than from an actual treatment. In contrast, the "Nocebo Effect" refers to the harm caused to the body due to the belief that a medicine or treatment is damaging, as seen in the example of the man attempting suicide.

The four stories we have mentioned above demonstrate the significant influence that our beliefs can exert on our bodies. However, this does not necessarily mean that believing in anything will automatically make it come true. For instance, the belief of the warship's commander did not transform the lighthouse into a ship. Similarly, having a strong belief that you will become wealthy or famous does not guarantee that it will manifest in reality. Nevertheless, what remains certain is that your mental state affects your body and behavior crucially.

* Note: In essence, while mindset can indeed play a significant role in shaping our psychological and physical states, the relationship between belief and its impact on the body and psyche is more complex and nuanced than a simple cause-and-effect relationship.

63

## Summary

Belief forms the basis of human behavior. If someone believes strongly in something, it can influence their thoughts, emotions, and behaviors, which in turn can also affect their overall well-being.

1. To change someone's behavior, one must first convince them of the truth, gain their faith in it, and then encourage them to act on it.

2. Misunderstanding the world leads to incorrect actions.

3. Our mindset impacts both our psychological and physical states. If you convince someone of something, their body and psyche might follow.

# Einstein Pattern

If something refuses to change, everything else must cope.

# Einstein Pattern

When he was only sixteen years old, Einstein had a weird question: "What if he could move with a light beam?" For example, if he moved at the same speed and alongside a light beam, what would he observe? Because light travels in waves, he should observe a light wave similar to, for example, a sea wave. However, Einstein found it very confusing that there was no such thing as a stationary light wave.

As he grew older, Einstein began to consider other mental experiments that did not require any complicated tools, only a sharp mind and a bit of imagination. One of the most important experiments he thought about was the experiment of magnets and current, which he later presented in a simpler way.

Imagine a man standing at a railway station (in the black shirt). When a train passed in front of the station, the man saw the train struck by lightning from both the front and back sides at the same moment. Einstein wondered, if there was another man riding on that train, what would that man see?

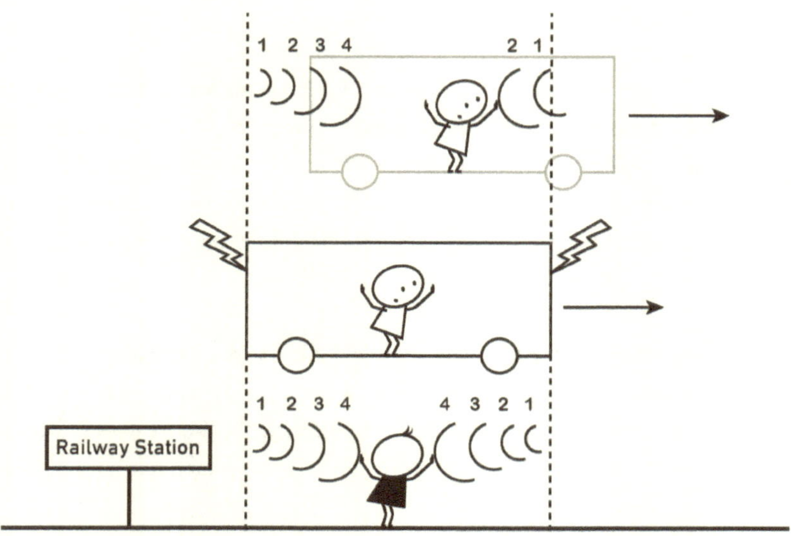


At first glance, one might think, "The man inside the train will likewise witness the lightning strike the train from the front and back sides at the same moment, just like the standing man saw." However, there is an issue with the constant speed of light; it does not change. As a result, the man inside the train will observe the first beam of light strike the train from the front and then, after a moment, the second beam of light strike the train from the back. Thus, he will not see lightning strike on both sides of the train at the same moment like the standing man did. The two observers will perceive different things. This scenario illustrates how the fundamental principles of physics, like the constancy of the speed of light, can lead to unexpected outcomes.

## Further Explanation

In this scenario, two observers are present: one stands on the platform (wearing a black shirt), and another is aboard a moving train. They both witness the same events—the lightning strikes hitting the front and back of the train. However, due to their relative motion, they perceive these events differently:

The observer on the platform sees the lightning strikes as simultaneous because the light from both strikes reaches them at the same time. For simplicity, let's say it takes "4 seconds," as shown in the last picture.

On the other hand, the observer on the moving train sees the lightning strike at the front of the train first. This is because the train is moving towards the light from that strike, causing it to take less time to reach the observer, let's say, "2 seconds". The lightning strike at the back of the train is observed later, as the train is moving away from the light of that strike. Thus, it takes more time to reach the observer "6 seconds".

This difference in the perception of simultaneity illustrates the concept of relative simultaneity, where the order of events depends on the observer's frame of reference. It challenges our intuitive understanding of time as an absolute, fixed entity and instead demonstrates that the order of events can be relative to an observer's motion.

Einstein's thought experiment along with others played a crucial role in the development of the special theory of relativity and later the general theory of relativity. it revealed that time and space are intertwined into a four-dimensional spacetime fabric, and the measurement of time and distance depends on the relative motion between observers.

## The Special Theory of Relativity

This thought experiment led Einstein to propose the theory of special relativity in 1905, which revolutionized our understanding of space, time, and motion, and became one of the cornerstones of modern physics. Later, Einstein further extended these ideas to the theory of general relativity. Both theories have undergone extensive testing and consistently enjoy support from experimental evidence.

The result of the thought experiment is puzzling. The observer standing on the platform sees the beams striking simultaneously, while the man on the train perceives them striking separately. According to the special theory of relativity, each individual has a different time frame, and there is no absolute truth about the two events.

## Light versus Normal Objects

Assume a man stands on the road, and a stopped car shoots a cannon at him with a projectile speed of 100 kilometers per hour. The man would mostly die upon impact. Now, consider if the car moves away from the man at the same speed as the bullet. In this case, the bullet instantly falls to the ground without reaching the man, as the opposing speeds result in zero velocity.

Now, let's consider the opposite scenario: if the car moves towards the man at 100 km/h and fires the cannon, the bullet's speed becomes 200 kilometers per hour (adding the car's speed). This makes it even more fatal.

In summary, when two objects move in opposing directions, their velocities are subtracted (car going forward, shot going backward). When they move in the same direction, velocities are added (both moving forward), according to classical physics laws set by Isaac Newton. However, these laws were challenged by Einstein's new theory of relativity.

If we were to replace the cannon with a flashlight on the car, then, according to Newton's previous laws, we would need to calculate the speed of light by adding the car's speed to the speed of light when the car is moving forward in the direction of light. Conversely, we would subtract the speeds if the car is moving backward in the opposite direction to the light.

Given that the speed of light is approximately 300,000 kilometers per hour, if the car is moving forward at 100,000 km/h, the speed of the light beam should theoretically increase to 400,000 km/h. Similarly, if the car is moving backward, the speed of the light beam should decrease to 200,000 km/h. However, experimental results have shown that the speed of light remains constant, regardless of whether the car is moving forward or backward. Light does not behave like a cannonball in this context, and this inconsistency raises a significant challenge within the realm of the laws of physics.

## Another Perspective

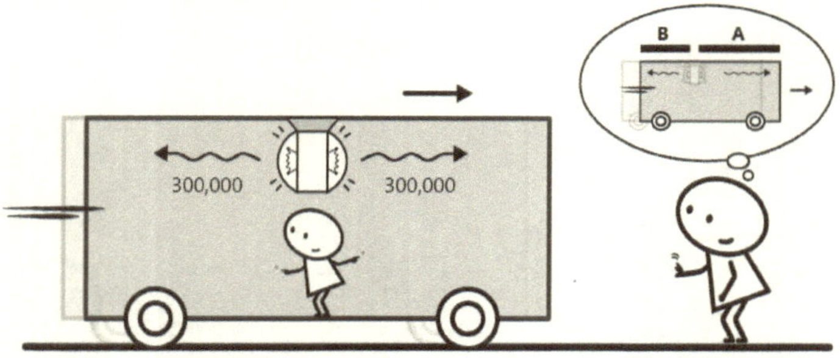


For more clarification, let's illustrate the experiment from another perspective. Imagine a passenger inside a train firing a flashlight both forward and backward simultaneously.

This will lead also to a contradiction. The person inside the train sees both light beams reaching the sides of the train simultaneously, but the observer at the station, due to the constant speed of light, sees the light reaching the back of the train first and then the front. Because, for him, the two beams travel different distances (the line A is longer than B). This means that each person has their own "time frame," and the order of events can differ for each.

The law (speed = distance / time) comes into focus here. Both people, "on the train" and "at the station," observe the constant speed of light, but the distance traveled by light differs for each of them. This creates a paradox: how can the speed remain constant while the distance varies? To preserve the equation, time must increase as the distance increases, resulting in "motion slowing down." This concept is known as the "special theory of relativity." It explains that light has a constant speed even when traveling different distances, challenging a fundamental law of physics. As a result, time must stretch out to maintain logical consistency.

While the theory is famously known as the "Theory of Relativity," Albert Einstein believed it should be named the "Theory of Invariance" because that concept is at its core.

## Relativity for a Ten-Year-Old Child

Simplifying topics for children is a good practice, even for oneself. We know that the area of a rectangle is given by the simple law: (Area = length × width). For example, if Sarah has a rectangle with a length of "4 units" and a width of "3 units," the area will be "12 square units."

Now, let's imagine Tariq sees the same rectangle and is assured its area is "16 square units." And length is "4 units." This leads to a problem: either the law is wrong or Tariq must see the width differently. There's no other explanation. So, the width of the rectangle must be "4 units," for Tariq instead of three, and that means the width is relative and not fixed; it changes for each observer depending on their position or state.

This example, although not real, illustrates the logical contradiction that led to the special theory of relativity. It demonstrates why we need to stretch time, much like a rubber band, in order to preserve what is most fundamental – which is 'logic.' We cannot sacrifice logic for anything else.

Similarly, speed is a product of time and distance. If the speed stays constant universally, then the other two factors must be relative.

## The Invariant Principle

The "invariant principle," the core of Einstein's thinking pattern, is exemplified in the following scenario: Can we cover the entire chessboard shown above (excluding the two corners) with dominoes? Testing this by placing dominos one by one is an option, but a simpler approach is to apply the invariant principle.

Each domino covers one black and one white square, regardless of its placement. So, with ten dominos, we have 10 black and 10 white squares covered—this is an "invariant" property. However, the board has 30 white squares and 32 black squares, making it impossible to cover the board entirely with dominoes.

The invariant principle provides us with the answer without exhaustive testing. For things to remain consistent, other elements must conform.

74

## Summary


1. In any coherent system, variables must be capable of logically varying in relation to each other. However, when one variable remains absolutely constant in all situations, the other variables must be relative, rather than absolute, to maintain consistency.

2. Logical consistency is fundamental and cannot be compromised.

3. Thought experiments can lead to the creation of new theories and ideas.

75

# Inverted Sock Pattern

If no solution is found in this world, turn the world upside-down.

# Inverted Sock Pattern

This thinking technique originates from Einstein's second significant thought experiment is about gravity. The Earth's attraction to objects has always seemed mysterious and unlike magnet attraction, which only applies to metals. However, Earth's gravity affects everything, making it more complex than magnetism. Additionally, gravity is much weaker compared to magnetic forces. If Earth's gravity were as strong as a magnet, it would be impossible to walk on its surface. So, the question arises: What is the secret of gravity?

Before we dive into the theory of gravity, we should understand that this is not a mathematical invention. Even a bright twelve-year-old kid could grasp the thinking that gave rise to the theory of general relativity. It isn't the result of complex mathematical reasoning. The theory is undoubtedly revolutionary, but its essence can be understood by anyone.

One might question why physicists need to know advanced mathematics. The answer lies in using mathematical equations to prove and validate hypotheses rather than to create them, especially in thought experiments; imagination and reasoning are the keys to developing groundbreaking theories like general relativity. The distinction between theories and their mathematical formulations is akin to the difference between a man and his shadow. Knowing a man is more important than understanding how his shadow behaves.

In Einstein's mental experiment, he envisioned a scenario where a man is inside an elevator, and suddenly the elevator's cord is cut, causing the man to fall freely.

During this fall, the man experiences weightlessness, as if he's floating in the air inside the elevator, with Earth's gravity seemingly disappearing. If the elevator abruptly halts, the man falls back to the floor and regains his weight. From this experiment, Einstein drew an unconventional conclusion: What if gravity doesn't mysteriously drag us down but, instead, we are "falling" down an incline, and this fall is what pushes us down to the Earth, causing us to feel our weight? In essence, falling down and gravity are two sides of the same coin.

I wish you could see the beauty of this realization: Earth's gravity, which draws everything towards its surface, is actually a consequence of a curvature in space, causing objects to literally fall towards the Earth.

Einstein's "general theory of relativity" suggests that large bodies like Earth, planets, and stars create a curvature in the fabric of space-time. Imagine placing a heavy metallic ball on a sheet of cloth; the curvature created by the ball causes everything to fall towards it. Similarly, the presence of Earth curves the fabric of space-time, making everything nearby, such as the moon, slide down towards Earth. Henceforth, gravity is no longer a mystical force but a consequence of space-time curvature.

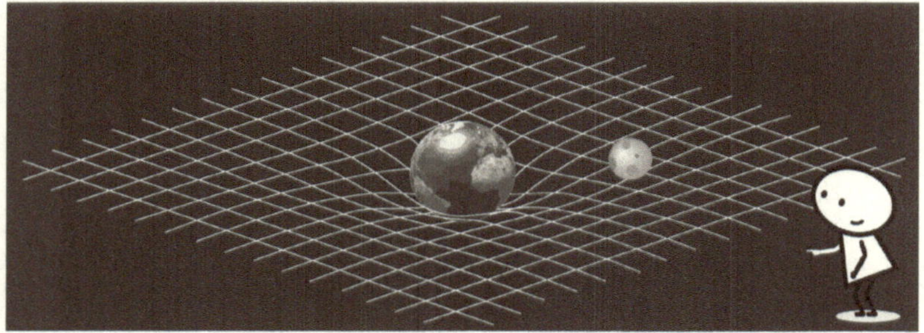

because the Earth is bending the fabric of the space, the moon is falling towards it.

Regarding the moon not falling on Earth, it remains in a stable orbit due to its fast rotation, which generates a centrifugal force—an apparent force arising from its inertia—that balances the curvature sliding force. This equilibrium prevents planets from falling into the sun as well. A simple example can be seen when a boy rotates a bucket of water; it doesn't spill because the centrifugal force counteracts gravity. This delicate cosmic dance of gravitational pull and centrifugal force keeps celestial bodies suspended in equilibrium.

In this book, we aren't studying scientific discoveries; instead, we seek to extract the underlying thinking techniques behind them. What patterns of thinking can we learn from Einstein's approach to solving analogous problems?

## Inverted Sock Metaphor

The "Inverted Sock" metaphor represents an advanced thinking pattern. Imagine feeling a small stone hurting your foot inside your shoe. After taking off the shoe and not finding the stone, you deduce it might be inside the sock. This realization leads you to remove the stone, bringing relief.

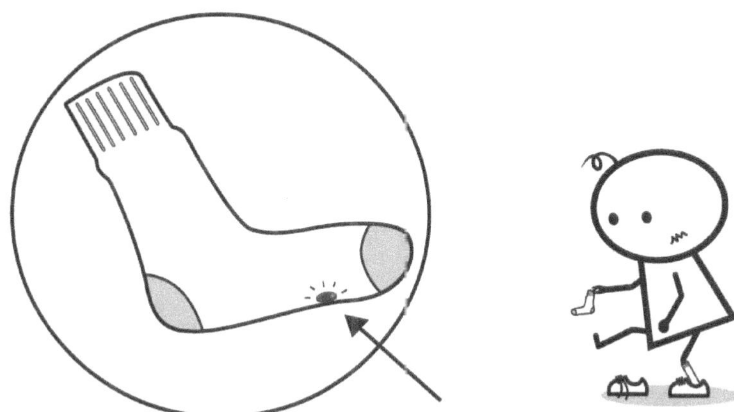

Similarly, in the world of problem-solving, we sometimes face challenges that cannot be resolved using our current understanding (outside the sock model). To find the real solution, we must shift our entire perspective (inside the sock model) and explore a new world view. This process, known as a "Paradigm Shift," is crucial for tackling gravity-like problems.

Three key concepts play a role: the "outside the sock model," the "inside the sock model," and the "pebble" (the underlying problem). In reality, the "inside the sock" model often remains hidden, as dominant theories become deeply ingrained beliefs over time. For example, the long-held belief was that gravity is a mysterious ethereal force floating in space (the outside of the sock model). However, Einstein's "curvature interpretation" revealed the truth: gravity is not a force, but rather a fall down a curved path (the inside of the sock model).

Einstein's approach involved viewing the mysterious force of gravity as an apparent effect of something else in an alternative mental model of the universe. This led to a paradigm shift, where he conceived that large objects bend the space-time fabric, causing smaller objects to fall towards them; this is the reality of gravity.

Such epistemological paradigm shifts are rare in the history of science, occurring only a few times in physics. Nonetheless, this method of thinking remains valuable, allowing us to apply the shift to micro-world problems, like the following example, instead of the entire universe model. However, achieving a transformation of the entire scientific paradigm could potentially earn someone the Nobel Prize someday.

## The Circular Room Story

In Yakov Perelman's classic book "Physics for Entertainment" from 1913, there is a narrative that I've edited as follows:

Your billionaire friend, Hassan, resides in a magnificent mansion in France and has graciously invited you to spend the summertime with him. Hassan has a penchant for peculiar buildings and often imports architectural models from all over the world. He's excited to show you his latest addition, the magical ball-shaped room in his house. As you enter the room and close the door behind you, you notice it's shaped like a hollow ball with a few pieces of furniture inside. After a while, you discover something bizarre: with just the movement of your feet, you can roll the entire room for a few meters. It feels like you're inside a light bubble or balloon, and as you walk in any direction, the entire room rolls accordingly. You are left perplexed, wondering how this could be possible since the room is heavy and constructed from concrete. Before reading the solution, take a moment to ponder how the room is rolling under Hassan's feet as he walks inside it.

## The Solution:

1. Initially, everyone who enters the room experiences the phenomenon of the room rolling in all directions for a few meters. This is the world we are familiar with and accustomed to —the "outside-sock world."

2. Now, let's apply Einstein's thinking method and delve deeper into the phenomenon. Is it possible that the apparent room rolling is an effect of something else? Could there be an alternative explanation for the sensation?

3. The answer is yes. Consider this: if we could walk upwards along the curved wall for a few steps, we would experience the feeling of rolling. However, this would only be possible if the room is rapidly rotating around its vertical axis.

4. Thus, if the room's floor is spinning at a high speed around a vertical axis, we can walk a few feet on the walls due to centrifugal force, the same force that keeps water from flowing out of a bucket when it's spun

forcefully. When we walk against the wall, it creates the illusion that we are standing on the ground while the room is rolling under our feet, resembling a ball on a slope. In essence, there are two world models at play here: one represents the apparent reality of the room rolling, and the other is the actual reality; the centrifugal force allowing the man to step on the wall.

The ingenious aspect of this scenario lies in the fact that the two worlds share a common element—something that is real on one side while being merely an effect on the other. This is analogous to the "stone in the sock" example. In the room story, the deceptive event is the room rolling, while the actual cause exists on the opposite side of our mental model—the centrifugal force.

It's important to note that the room is designed to spin smoothly, with all the furniture fixed to the floor, ensuring that the person inside doesn't feel the rotation itself.

## Paradigm Shift

We proposed the concept of the "inverted sock" for simplicity. However, in the philosophy of science, we find the term "the paradigm shift" or "the change of the cognitive paradigm." Thomas Kuhn coined this term in his 1962 book, "The Structure of Scientific Revolutions." According to Kuhn, the history of science follows these cycles:

First, there is "standard science," which employs a heuristic model to describe the universe, like Newton's theory, which portrays it as a mechanical machine. Within this prevailing science, new findings and small inventions emerge. The theory dominates the minds of scientists and the public for extended periods, sometimes spanning millennia.

However, at certain points in history, abnormal problems arise that defy solutions within the prevailing standard theory, leading to a crisis in science. At such moments, the stage is set for a revolution where the old standard theory is replaced by an entirely new perception of reality. Einstein's introduction of the general theory of relativity exemplifies such a paradigm shift, moving away from the Newtonian view of the universe as a mechanical absolute clock to a new relative perspective.

This cycle of "dilemma-revolution" repeats throughout history, as new theories replace old ones, becoming the new "standard science" with their guiding models. Eventually, new issues emerge that challenge the capabilities of the current theory, necessitating another paradigm shift, and so on. This continuous evolution with radical fluctuations characterizes the progress of science.

It is essential to recognize that a paradigm shift doesn't directly tackle the immediate issue at hand; rather, it orchestrates a profound transformation of the entire conceptual framework that envelops it. This transformative process can occasionally result in the spontaneous resolution of the problem being addressed. Such paradigm shifts are infrequent occurrences, as they stand as formidable challenges to the prevailing comprehension of the cosmos, demanding extraordinary intellectual capacities for their realization.

These pivotal shifts in perspective are exceptional occurrences, as they inherently challenge and even overturn the established perceptions governing our understanding of the universe. They necessitate a level of cognitive prowess that extends beyond the norm. Only groundbreaking theories possess the potential to usher in such paradigm shifts, akin to the theory of relativity. This revolutionary theory not only upended the foundations of physics but also fundamentally reconfigured our entire conception of the cosmos itself.

84

Additionally, the new epistemological model generated by the paradigm shift often offers solutions to previously unconsidered problems. However, this style of thinking is not viable for all situations and is required when all known approaches have reached a dead end. "The paradigm shift" serves as the driving force behind the most radical scientific revolutions.

## Summary

The "Inverted Sock Method," or more formally, "Paradigm Shift," involves the following steps:

1. Identify the problem or phenomenon that requires explanation, such as "gravity" or "the sensation of the room rolling beneath your feet."

2. Consider whether this phenomenon is not what it appears to be but an effect of something else.

3. Ask yourself what else could potentially cause a similar effect or phenomenon.

4. If you discover the true cause, adjust your entire worldview model, turning it upside down like turning over a sock, to accommodate the new understanding and align with your findings.

By following these steps, you can develop a new model of reality in which the problem becomes more apparent and solvable, leading to a paradigm shift in your previous knowledge.

# Scientific Research Pattern

The secret lies in one word: Consistency.

# Scientific Research Pattern

Scientific research can be roughly defined with the following definition: "It is the study of a phenomenon to understand, control, and predict." While scientific research may lead to innovation in the form of new inventions or theories, in this chapter, we use the term scientific research to refer to ordinary logical thinking rather than unconventional thinking.

The reader may wonder why we are discussing a "regular" method of thinking while we are supposed to focus on unconventional strategies in this book. The reason for this is that in order to grasp thinking strategies beyond common sense, you must first understand the boundaries of conventional thinking. This contrast can be beneficial to distinguish between standard and unusual thinking. In such direct reasoning, there are no sophisticated hacks or twists; you simply use the thread of logic to connect and weave the facts in order to arrive at a solution.

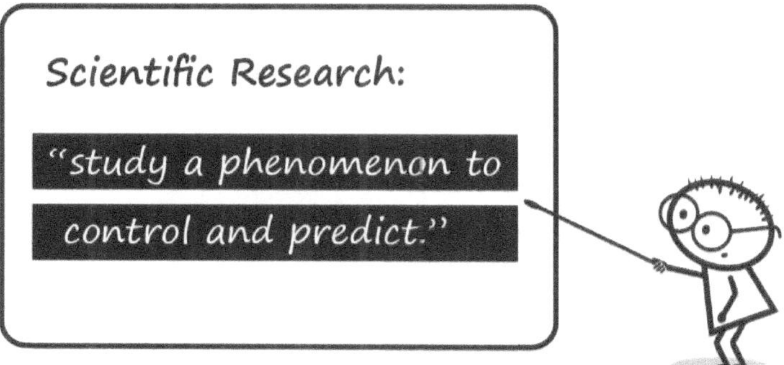

In the above figure, the researcher, named Noor, observed a butterfly flying as indicated by the arrows. However, the butterfly disappeared from Noor's sight in the blank areas, leaving him clueless about its movement.

Nevertheless, Noor has an "intuition" that the butterfly flew in a zigzag line. In scientific research, we label this intuition "the research hypothesis." Recognizing that intuition is inherently "subjective," the researcher must validate it with real data. For instance, Noor can conduct experiments or employ logical and mathematical analyses to verify the accuracy of his intuition. Only then can the intuition transform into an "objective" fact.

Note that While intuition is inherently subjective and not considered scientific in nature, it plays a crucial role in motivating scientific inquiry and guiding researchers in deciding what to test.

Noor should validate his intuition by providing evidence along the dashed lines on the coming figure through one of the following approaches:

(1) Conducting experiments, (2) Employing pure reasoning, or (3) Citing quotes from other researchers.

For instance, Noor conducted an experiment that demonstrated the butterfly had indeed flown from point B to point C. Then, using logical arguments, he established that the butterfly had flown from point C to point D. Additionally, Noor obtained supporting evidence from another researcher who had previously shown the butterfly's trajectory along the dashed line from D to E. Finally, through further reasoning, Noor proved that the butterfly had indeed flown along the path from point F to point G.

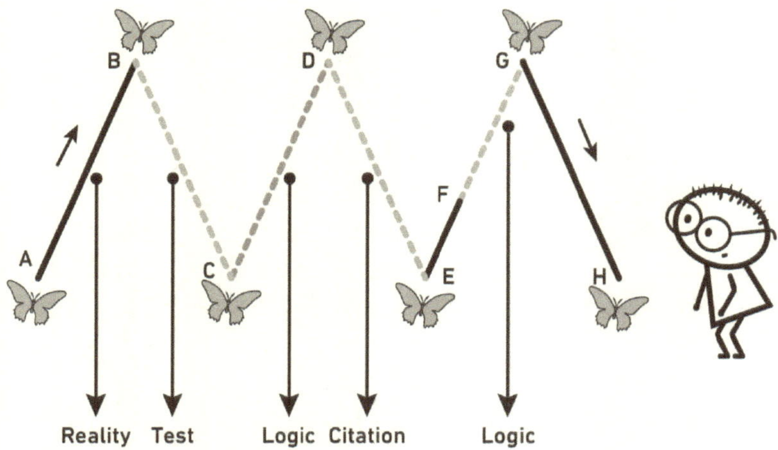


The cumulative efforts of these approaches validated Noor's initial idea that the butterfly flies "in the form of a zigzag line." Indeed, in some cases, a single method, such as an experiment or reasoning, could be sufficient to prove the entire hypothesis.

In the end, the collaborative synergy of diverse methodologies solidified the notion that the butterfly's flight was indeed governed by the zigzag principle. By meticulously analyzing the angles and distances between each successive point, Noor revealed a pattern that transcended mere randomness. Moreover, his collaborative approach extended to seeking feedback from experts in the field, whose insights further bolstered the credibility of his findings. This multi-faceted validation exemplified the potency of a multidisciplinary approach in scientific inquiry.

Let's consider another scenario where Noor lacks any intuition, leaving him without a hypothesis to begin with. In this situation, Noor must test all the grey points in the illustration below to determine the path the butterfly took. Such exhaustive testing is referred to as the "framework." When we have no initial hunch about what to do, having a framework becomes essential as it provides a structured space for conducting experiments. Indeed, testing an entire framework would be more difficult than testing a certain hypothesis.

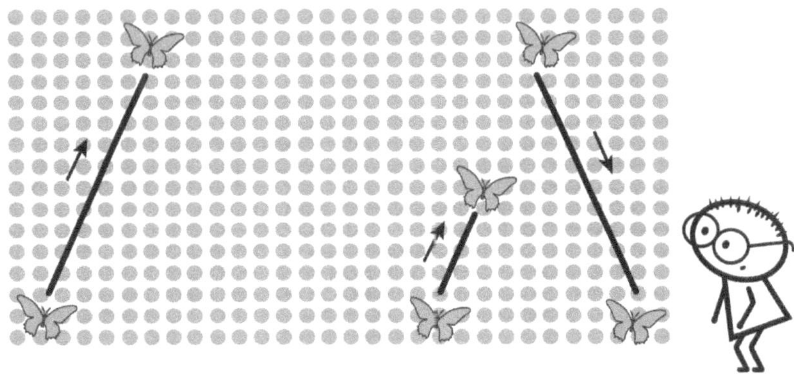

Similar to the hypothesis, the entire framework can also undergo testing through various means, including logic, experiments, and references to findings from other scholars. These methods can be used individually or combined to assess and validate the comprehensive framework.

## When there is No Framework

The framework plays a crucial role in indicating where tests should be conducted and specifying the types of those tests. In our example, the grey dots mark the locations where we must test to determine if the butterfly has passed through those points. Having a well-defined framework is indispensable in scientific research, as it provides boundaries even when we lack intuition, guiding us towards potential solutions.

However, in the absence of a framework to approach a problem, it not only hinders our ability to solve the problem but also prevents us from even designing experiments to seek a solution. One such question in science that lacks a general framework is the "consciousness problem." The nature of consciousness and how it occurs remain elusive and mysterious. We do not only lack knowledge of "what the answer is," but we also lack a starting point—a framework—to explore this enigmatic domain. Problems without any framework are among the most challenging ones in the realm of science.

## What is Logic?

Logic serves as the bedrock upon which rational discourse and scientific inquiry are built, enabling us to navigate the complexities of the world with clarity and coherence. We can describe it as a series of interconnected ideas that fit together like puzzle pieces to arrive at a new truth. Three fundamental characteristics define logic: (1) ideas must be objective, (2) ideas must be connected, and (3) ideas must be consistent.

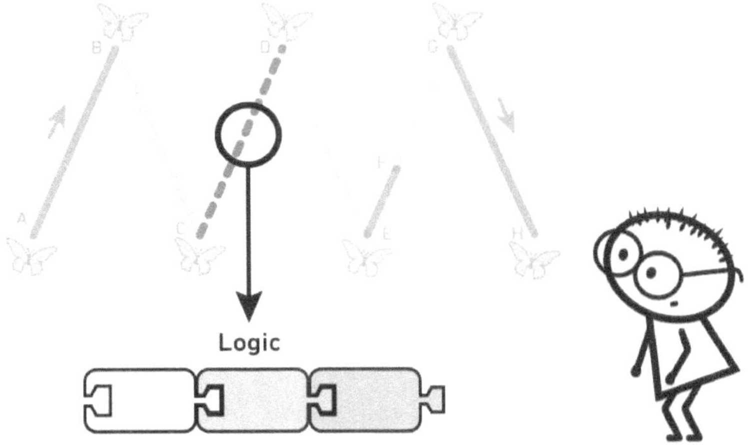


## Let's Examine the Following Simple Examples

Statement 1: "The cow's milk increases due to the rain increasing."
This statement lacks linkage in its logic since the connection between the rain and the increase in milk is not clear. A more accurate and connected statement could be: "Increasing rain leads to an expansion of grazing land, providing better nourishment to the cows, resulting in an increase in the amount of milk they produce."

Statement 2: "I believe that milk increases in autumn."
This phrase lacks the "objectivity" condition. While personal beliefs and certainty may exist, logical statements avoid relying on subjective thoughts. A more objective statement could be: "Historical data shows an increase in milk production during the autumn due to favorable environmental conditions and diet changes for the cows."

Statement 3: "The increase in rainfall enhances milk quality."
This statement exhibits "inconsistency" and lacks coherence since the term "increase" refers to the amount of rain, and its direct relationship with the quality of milk remains unclear. A more consistent statement could be: "Studies indicate a positive correlation between higher rainfall and improved grazing land, which, in turn, positively influences the quality of milk produced by the cows."

## Example 2

Tariq is taller than Saleh, and Emad is shorter than Tariq. Which of the following sentences is correct?

(a) Saleh is slightly taller than Emad.
(b) Emad is barely taller than Saleh.
(c) Emad and Saleh are equal in height.
(d) We don't know who is taller, Saleh or Emad.

This is a straightforward logic question, yet it might appear difficult and confusing due to the inconsistency of terms, which can distract short-term memory. Consequently, one might feel the need to use pen and paper to solve it. However, unifying the comparison using the term "shorter," for example, transforms the sentence into: "Saleh is shorter than Tariq, and Emad is shorter than Tariq." This simplification makes it easier to solve without the necessity of writing down facts.

## Example 3

This question was presented by the Udacity website as part of an educational scholarship test: Four children (David, Sarah, Ali, and Amber) participated in a race to determine the fastest among them. Each child was wearing something unique (a red shirt, a hat, sunglasses, and a scarf). Let us consider the following statements: The kid in the red shirt completed the race before David but after the kid in the hat. Amber wears sunglasses. The kid wearing the scarf finished the race late. Sarah completed the race before the sunglasses kid. Ali doesn't wear a hat. Who won the race?

## Solution

To find out who won the race, we can use direct reasoning and proceed step-by-step; focusing on one piece of information at a time makes things consistent and clear. Let's attempt to solve it using memory:

- First, consider David: He finished after the child in the hat but before the child in the red shirt. Thus, David doesn't wear a shirt or a hat.

- Amber wears sunglasses, so David cannot be wearing them. Hence, he must be wearing the scarf.

- Since the child wearing the scarf finished late, David must have been the last to finish the race.

- Sarah finished before the child with sunglasses, which means Amber is excluded from being the winner.

- Ali doesn't wear a hat, scarf, or sunglasses, so he must be wearing the red shirt.

- As Ali finished after the child in the hat, he is also eliminated from being the winner.

- Therefore, the winner of the race is Sarah.

The key to solving this type of problem is to focus on one aspect at a time, gradually eliminating possibilities until an answer emerges. To put it another way, we aim for "consistency" first to make the issue more manageable.

| David | |
|---|---|
| shirt | 1 |
| hat | 2 |
| glasses | 3 |
| scarf | 4 |

| Sarah | |
|---|---|
| shirt | 1 |
| hat | 2 |
| glasses | 3 |
| scarf | 4 |

| Ali | |
|---|---|
| shirt | 1 |
| hat | 2 |
| glasses | 3 |
| scarf | 4 |

| Amber | |
|---|---|
| shirt | 1 |
| hat | 2 |
| glasses | 3 |
| scarf | 4 |

## Archimedes Story

The story of Archimedes is one of the most notable examples of coherent logical reasoning (287 B.C.). Archimedes was a mathematician, engineer, and inventor, widely regarded as one of the most influential scientists of all time. According to the legend, "King Hero II" commissioned a goldsmith to create a gold crown and provided enough gold for the task. The goldsmith fulfilled the request, but the king grew suspicious of the goldsmith's honesty, fearing that he might have substituted some gold with a cheaper metal like copper. To verify the purity of the crown, the king sought after the expertise of Archimedes, a trusted advisor and scientist.

## The Solution:

For simplicity, let's assume the gold given by the king was one kilogram. The easiest way to determine the crown's purity would be to weigh it. Archimedes weighed the crown, and it appeared to be one kilogram. However, this alone was not sufficient evidence, as the goldsmith could have replaced some gold with another substance while maintaining the weight.

Archimedes had to devise another solution. Gold is distinguished from other metals by its "density." Gold has a higher density than copper or silver. Density and volume are inversely related, as shown in the picture. For instance, if we compare the volume of sponge and wood of equal weight, the sponge has a larger volume because it is less dense than wood. Archimedes realized that instead of weighing the crown, he should measure its volume.

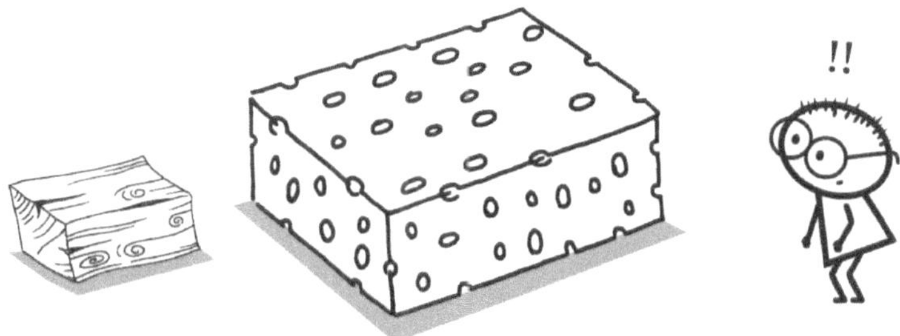

Because wood is denser, a gram of wood is smaller than a gram of sponge.

A straightforward way to do this was to melt down the crown and shape it into a square block, then compare its volume to a similar one-kilogram pure gold block. However, this approach would destroy the crown itself.

The question then became, "How can we compare the volume of the crown to the volume of a kilo of pure gold without damaging the crown?"

While pondering this problem during a bath, Archimedes noticed that when he immersed his body in the bathtub, the water level rose and his weight decreased. This observation led to a breakthrough: the body displaces an equal volume of water, making it lighter. Archimedes realized that he could use water displacement to measure the volume of objects without damaging them.

By immersing the crown in water, a volume of water equal to the crown's volume would rise. By collecting this displaced water, Archimedes could then submerge a pure gold ingot in water and measure the water it displaces. By comparing the two volumes of displaced water — the crown's and the ingot's — he could determine whether the crown was pure gold or combined with another metal. After conducting the experiment, Archimedes discovered that the crown was not made of pure gold, as its volume was larger than that of a gold crown. The goldsmith's deception was revealed, and according to the story, the goldsmith lost his life as a penalty for his cheating.

The narrative of Archimedes serves as an excellent example of employing coherent reasoning to arrive at a solution. The drawing above illustrates how facts are logically linked, like puzzle pieces, leading from point A to point D.

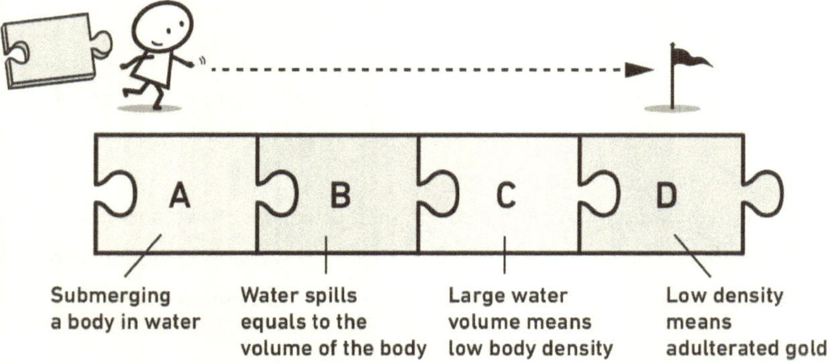


## Retrograde Analysis (Backward Thinking)

We typically solve logic problems by starting from the premises and reaching a conclusion. However, there are instances where considering the premises from the opposite perspective proves to be more effective. Let's explore this idea with the following example.

Imagine we have the six cards displayed above turned upside down, and each person has to randomly choose one. The person with the highest number on their card wins. Now, after the draw, you find that you have the card with the number two, and the second player also has a card. The second player proposes swapping cards with you. Would you be willing to accept the offer?

Considering that you have obtained a lower number, "2," switching your card with the second player's card makes your chances of obtaining a higher number, 4:1 ("3, 4, 5, 6" to "1"). Thus, trading cards seems to be in your favor.

**The Solution:**

Before hastily accepting this offer, let's approach the issue inversely; from the perspective of the second player who proposed the card swap: If the other player possessed the card 6, he wouldn't have suggested the swap, as he would have the highest card already. Similarly, if he had the card 5, he wouldn't swap either, as he would think the chances of you having a lower card are higher (1, 2, 3, 4) compared to (6). The same reasoning applies to the number 4; he would perceive the probability of you having a lower number (1, 2, 3) as higher than the two possibilities of you having a higher number (5, 6). Hence, he wouldn't propose the swap. Now, if the other player had the card 3, he would consider the likelihood of you having a higher number (4, 5, 6) versus (1, 2), which makes it ideal for him to swap with us. However, we should be aware that he knows if we get card 6, we will decline the swap. Thus, the possibilities in the other player's mind are (4, 5) versus (1, 2), which are equal, leading to no sense in offering the swap.

From this analysis, we can deduce that the second player might have the card (1), and therefore, we shouldn't accept the swap.

## Retrograde Example 2

A strain of bacteria, initially consisting of "thousand bacteria," doubles in population every 24 hours. After sixty days, the bacteria population filled the entire lake. The question is, when was the lake half full?

Solution

Although the question may seem to require complex algebra, reading it backward from the fact that "the lake is half full" and considering that the bacteria double every day, we can deduce that this happened on the second to last day. Therefore, the lake was half full on the 59th day.

## Definition of Logic

Here is a somewhat formal definition of logic: "Logic is the science of how to think and reason correctly." Logic is a formal process that allows us to draw conclusions from existing knowledge. It begins with a known statement, referred to as a "premise," and leads to a newly derived piece of information, called the "conclusion."

## Types of Logical Reasoning

**- Deductive Reasoning:**

a)  All mountains are made of rocks.
b)  Kilimanjaro is a mountain.
c)  Therefore, Kilimanjaro is made of rocks.

In deductive reasoning, the truth of the premises (a, b) guarantees the truth of the conclusion (c). This top-down approach starts with general information and deduces a specific case. The derived conclusion is certain as long as the premises are true.

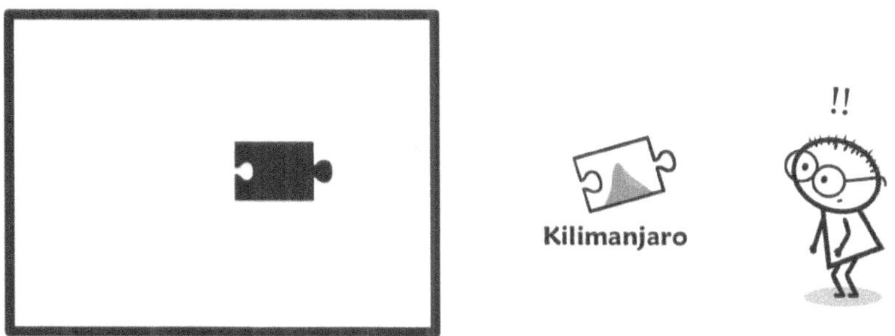


All mountains are made of rocks, implying that Kilimanjaro is made of rocks. This logic follows the principle of categorical syllogism, where the premise "All mountains are made of rocks" establishes a general category (mountains) and a characteristic (made of rocks). Applying this logic to Kilimanjaro, it can be inferred that Kilimanjaro, being a mountain, is also composed of rocks. This showcases how categorical statements can extend attributes to specific instances within a defined category.

## - Inductive Reasoning:

In this type of reasoning, the premises make the conclusion likely to be true but not entirely certain. For example:

a)  Every trial of Paracetamol shows that it relieves headache pain.
b)  Therefore, Paracetamol will relieve my headache pain.

The first premise, based on numerous experiments, leads us to conclude that Paracetamol should relieve everyone's headache pain, including ours. However, this conclusion is not entirely certain; there's a possibility that Paracetamol might not work for us. Inductive reasoning follows a bottom-up approach, starting with specific cases and generalizing the conclusion.

While deductive reasoning is more accurate, the scientific community often employs inductive reasoning, which is why science may not always be entirely precise.

## Summary

1. Scientific research thinking employs conventional methods, utilizing straight logic to reach solutions.

2. Logical thinking involves connecting facts like a series of puzzle pieces in a chain, leading from "premises" to valid "conclusions."

3. Retrograde analysis also starts from premises, yet it uses a different perspective, for example our opponent's, and traces backward to reach a conclusion.

4. Logical reasoning must be consistent, linked with no gaps, and objective to ensure coherence and validity.

## Appendix: Scientific Publishing

Imagine that you've conducted extensive research using the scientific reasoning outlined above. Your research has been carried out in a logical manner—connected, consistent, and objective. Through this process, you've discovered a unique cure for a rare disease, such as cancer. Now, the time has come to publish your findings and share them with the global scientific community. The process of writing and publishing your research should reflect the logical steps you undertook during your investigation. By meticulously detailing your methodology, data analysis, and the innovative principles underlying your cure, you ensure that the broader scientific community can fully comprehend, replicate, and build upon your groundbreaking work."

Using the IMRAD Method:

In 1977, the American National Standards Institute (ANSI) introduced the IMRAD model. This model, which originated in the late nineteenth century, has emerged as a widely accepted approach for publishing scientific papers and is now extensively employed in research publications worldwide. The acronym "IMRAD" stands for the following sections: Introduction, Method, Results, Analysis, and Discussion.

The Popularity of IMRAD:

The IMRAD structure has gained widespread popularity due to its inherent logical flow. A scientific study typically commences with a central question (identifying the problem), which is addressed in the "Introduction" section. Subsequently, the approach used to investigate the problem (research methods) is detailed in the "Method" section. The obtained outcomes (research results) are presented in the "Results" section. Finally, the implications and interpretations of these results (research analysis and discussion) are expounded upon in the respective sections.

By adhering to the IMRAD framework, you can effectively communicate your groundbreaking findings in a structured and coherent manner, ensuring that your research is comprehensible and impactful to the global scientific community.

The scientific research community comprises researchers who write scientific papers, editors and expert reviewers who assess manuscripts before publication in scientific journals, and a wider readership. The IMRAD model offers a unified structure for writing that facilitates seamless comprehension of papers, guiding readers from the problem statement to the proposed solution.

## Defining the Scientific Paper:

The book "How to Write and Publish a Scientific Paper" defines a scientific paper as follows:

- "A scientific paper is a written and published report describing original research results."

The authors of the book have supplemented this definition with an important condition: "the paper must be of high quality and adhere to a specific format." A scientific paper meeting these criteria becomes a primary intellectual product.

Consider the previous scenario, where you have dedicated a year to cancer research. When might it be pointless to publish a scientific paper?

A) Lack of Results: If your research yields no results, you don't have to write a scientific paper. Papers are not crafted to record or show research efforts but rather to convey findings.

B) Old known Results: There is no need to create a scientific paper if you generate outcomes that are already well-known and established. Papers are reserved mostly for novel and original contributions.

C) Secret Findings: Opting to keep new findings confidential prevents your work from qualifying as a scientific publication. Papers should be shared within the scientific community.

D) Mysterious Results: Discovering new results that cannot be replicated by others renders the research unpublishable. The Method section must detail the approach to enable reproducibility.

E) Strange Structure: Choosing a format other than the IMRAD approach or at least other standard format to present your results may lead to rejection, as unconventional formats can hinder comprehension.

F) Flawed Logic: If your argumentation is flawed or based on invalid reasoning, and the conclusion doesn't logically follow from the premises, your work may not be suitable for publication.

By considering these points, you can ensure that your research efforts align with the requirements for crafting a scientific paper and effectively contributing to the scientific community's knowledge.

# Opposites Pattern

If it is daylight, what comes after will certainly be a dark night.

# Opposites Pattern

In a fictional folklore tale inspired by Arabic or Italian mythology, the story revolves around an unjust king and a humble fisherman from the common people. The fisherman dares to propose marriage to the king's daughter, which the king perceives as an insult to his greatness. To punish the fisherman, the king arranges a lottery with two concealed stones in a bowl: one white and one black. If the fisherman draws the white stone, he will marry the daughter, but if he draws the black one, he will face death.

Despite warnings from the people, the fisherman remains steadfast and accepts the king's challenge. Unbeknownst to him, the king, who holds a deep grudge against the fisherman, places two identical white pebbles in the bowl, intending to exact revenge on his opponent.

On the day of the lottery, a crowd gathers to witness the outcome. The fisherman reaches into the bowl and swiftly swallows one of the pebbles, leaving everyone astonished and puzzled. They then check the second stone in the bowl, which turns out to be white, implying that the fisherman must have swallowed the black one. In reality, the fisherman had cleverly anticipated the king's scheme, ensuring his victory in the lottery and the fulfillment of his wish to marry the princess.

This simple tale conveys a valuable lesson about understanding the nature of things through their opposing aspects. The universe is replete with polar opposites such as day and night, negative and positive, and right and wrong. By recognizing one side of these dualities, we can deduce the other side. The fisherman's cunning approach exemplifies how one can make the most of situations involving paired opposites.

## The Strange Quantum Story

To discuss our upcoming story, we first need to grapple with a quandary in physics. In the 1920s, a revolutionary theory called "Quantum Mechanics" emerged, challenging our understanding of the world. At the macroscopic level, everything seems normal and predictable—cars, houses, and people behave according to classical physics. However, when we delve into the microscopic realm and examine the building blocks of our world, such as atoms, electrons, and neutrons, we encounter bizarre and mind-boggling phenomena.

One of the most peculiar aspects of Quantum Mechanics is the principle of "uncertainty," which posits that we cannot precisely determine the state of particles like electrons. To illustrate this, imagine a strange pen that could simultaneously exist in your bag and your pocket at the same moment. Or picture a cat that could be both in Khartoum with you and in Moscow with your sister, all at the same time. While such occurrences are confined to fairy tales, electrons and other subatomic particles can indeed display similar behavior.

To better grasp this concept, envision an electron as a spinning coin. It can spin either clockwise (up spin) or counterclockwise (down spin) around itself. The catch is that the electron can spin in both directions simultaneously, presenting a perplexing conundrum. How can something rotate in opposite directions at the same moment? Attempting to conceive of a coin rotating both from left to right and from right to left simultaneously seems utterly unimaginable.

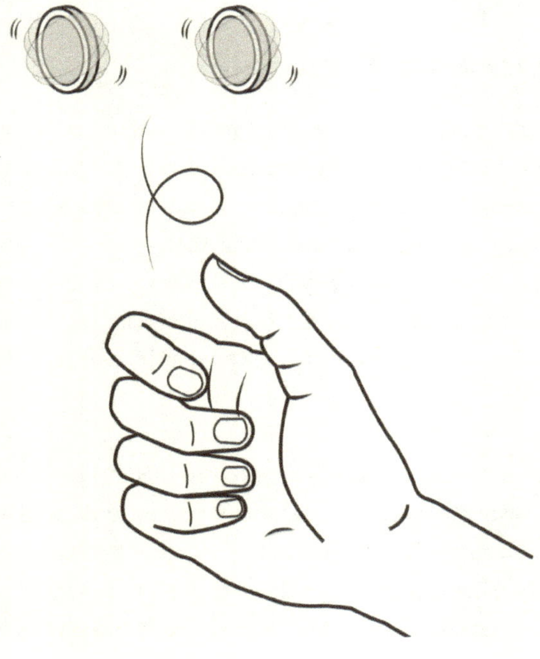

## The Dilemma of Entanglement

Another strange physics phenomenon is "quantum entanglement," which involves the connection of two particles, such as two electrons, in an opposite way. In simpler terms, if one particle spins up, the other spins down. To illustrate this, imagine tossing two coins in the air, as shown in the illustration above. When the first coin lands on the "tails" side, the second coin immediately lands on the "heads" side, even if you separate the two coins, placing one in Egypt and the other in France. They seem to fall on opposite sides as if they are somehow related. Are the two electrons communicating? How does the second electron always know what happens to the first one?

One of the proposed theories suggests that when one of the electrons spins up, it sends a signal to the other remote electron, causing it to spin down. However, this idea raises a problem because this phenomenon happens instantly, faster than the fastest thing in the universe—light. In physics, this is not acceptable, as it would violate the rule of causality, with information arriving before it was sent, which defies logic.

If a white ghost emerges in any of the boxes, a black ghost will instantly appear in the second box.

Einstein offered a simple yet smart solution to the "quantum entanglement" problem. His explanation proposed that there is no information transfer between the boxes—let's say one box is in America and the other in Japan—

containing the entangled electrons. Instead, the information already existed from the beginning, much like a pair of "right and left" gloves placed in separate boxes. When someone opens the first box in America and finds the left glove, they instantly identify the content of the second box in Japan as the right glove.

This explanation doesn't mean that information travels at great speed from one box to the other to communicate the glove's identity. The two gloves were already inherently opposite to each other, just like their nature as gloves.

For this explanation to hold, Einstein and his colleagues proposed the existence of a hidden variable. This variable appears at the moment of entanglement when the two particles connect, playing the role of the glove pair and holding the opposing information.

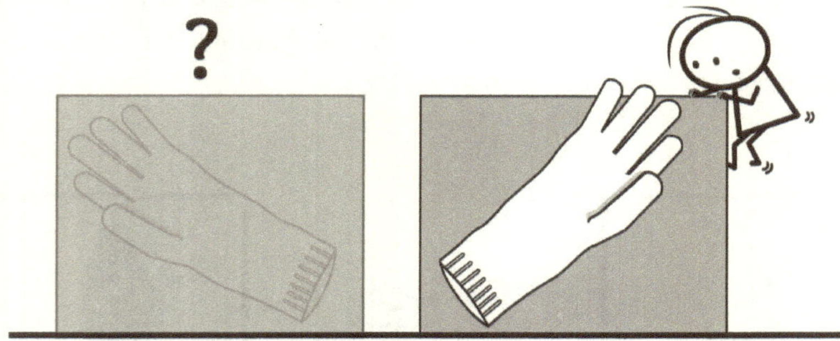


This perspective, shared by Einstein and the other two scientists, was outlined in a famous scientific publication titled "EPR," named after the three scientists. It suggested that quantum theory might be incomplete or incorrect. However, subsequent experiments have shown that Einstein and his colleagues were mistaken. The entanglement and the "information problem" still remain unsolved.

113

We now understand that information does not travel faster than light, yet two entangled particles seem to connect instantaneously in some mysterious way. Quantum physics continues to challenge our understanding of the universe, leaving the door open for other reasonable explanations of this phenomenon.

Despite the failure of Einstein and his colleagues' proposal, the "gloves" analogy remains a useful explanation for similar quandaries that teaching us a valuable and simple heuristic. Einstein, once again, enriches our thinking strategies, demonstrating that both simple and advanced thinking can lead to brilliant insights.

114

## Summary

1. The idea that two objects are always linked inversely suggests they may be natural counterparts, similar to a pair of gloves.

2. Access to one part of a pair can reveal a secret locked in the other part if they are inherently opposing each other.

3. If two things are naturally paired in opposition, their relationship doesn't require any communication channel to be explained.

# Hidden Dimension Pattern

When we encounter a deadlock, it can be a sign of a new dimension.

# Hidden Dimension Pattern

The story begins in the sixteenth century, and while it is about mathematics, you don't have to be a mathematician to appreciate and understand it. The lesson is always not the equations themselves but the pattern of thought that lies behind them.

During ancient times, scientists had the unusual habit of engaging in duel challenges to solve problems. If a scientist discovered a solution to an unknown equation, they would keep it to themselves, using it to challenge others for money rewards. One prominent mathematician of that era was "Cardan," who devised a method to solve all cubic equations. Cardan's method proved effective in solving most of those problems. However, some cubic equations, such as the one below, seem impossible to solve.

$$x^3 = 15x + 4$$

Whenever Cardan attempted to solve this equation, a square root of a negative number, $\sqrt{-121}$ would emerge within the steps. This indicated that the equation had no solution, as there is no such thing as "square root of a negative number." For example, we can calculate $\sqrt{9}$, but the calculation of $\sqrt{(-9)}$ is unknown. There is no real number that can be multiplied by itself to yield a negative nine.

Of course, Cardan and other mathematicians could have considered this equation unsolvable, but the problem was that everyone was certain the equation had a solution. For example, if you substitute the number 4 for X in the equation, you will find that it is one of the right answers:

$$64 = (15 \times 4) + 4$$

In algebra, any equation known as a "polynomial" like this one has solutions equal to the number of its exponents, and this is a fundamental rule. Therefore, besides the number 4, this equation must have two more solutions. However, finding these solutions posed a challenge due to the presence of the mysterious negative square root.

Before we investigate Cardan's problem that perplexed scientists, let's reflect on the origin of numbers. The concept of positive numbers is straightforward; for instance, "I have three apples" makes perfect sense. However, the ancient world struggled with the idea of "zero apples" or "negative three apples."

Initially, the concept of someone having a negative number of apples seemed unacceptable. But over time, ancient Egyptians discovered that negative numbers, such as (-3), were useful in calculating debts. It simply means that someone owes three apples.

Imagine a time when the world did not accept negative numbers. A simple equation like the one below, which resulted in the enigmatic (-1), was considered unsolvable:

$$x + 3 = 2$$

You might think the ancients were stupid, but the matter wasn't that simple. Consider this question two thousand years ago: "If you had two apples and took three apples from them, what would you have left?" The answer, according to our ancestors, was that this situation is impossible.

Similarly, the appearance of the negative square root in Cardan's equation remained a perplexing phenomenon, much like the ancient world's hesitation towards negative numbers. It was only later that Cardan's pupil, "Bombelli," introduced a groundbreaking novel idea: if the negative square root does not yield a positive or negative answer, then there may exist a new type of numbers yet to be discovered that can account for this negative root.

Bombelli proceeded to create this new type of numbers, written in the form $\sqrt{-1}$ and later known as "imaginary numbers," which are represented by the symbol ( $i$ ). Initially, this concept faced rejection, akin to the reluctance towards negative numbers in the past. Bombelli himself regarded the number he invented as a mere "workaround" to solve the Cardan equation.

$$x^3 = 15x + 4$$

$$x = \sqrt[3]{2 + \sqrt{-121}} + \sqrt[3]{2 - \sqrt{-121}}$$

$$x = \sqrt[3]{2 + 11\sqrt{-1}} + \sqrt[3]{2 - 11\sqrt{-1}}$$

Using his new number, Bombelli successfully solved the problem and obtained all three solutions:

$$4 \qquad -2 + \sqrt{3} \qquad -2 - \sqrt{3}$$

About two hundred years after the story of "Bombelli," $\sqrt{-1}$ has finally become a trustworthy number, confirming the existence of another dimension of numbers called "Imaginary Numbers," which are written in the letter form, (i, 2i, 3i...). Some scholars, like Gauss, say that the name "imaginary" is misleading because these are real-existing numbers.

Even if you are not a fan of math, you can still use the graphical method to understand the concept. Let's take the following example:

$$y = x^2 - 4$$

We can set $y$ to equal zero:

$$0 = x^2 - 4$$
$$4 = x^2$$

By solving for x, we find:

$$x = \pm 2$$

We can also get the values of x using the graph approach; as shown below, the curve of the equation (when y = zero) intersects with the horizontal axis at the points -2 and 2, which are the answers.

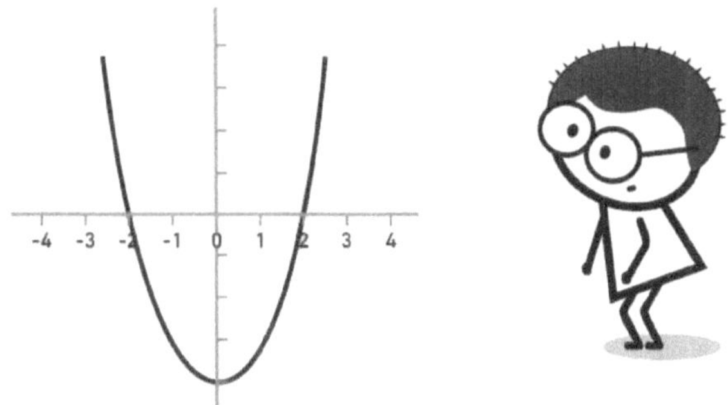


So either mathematically or graphically, we attain the same results.

## Now let's take another equation:

$$y = x^2 + 1$$

If we try to solve the equation mathematically, we get $x = \pm\sqrt{-1}$ but when we try to solve it graphically, we get the figure below. We know the solution is where the curve intersects the horizontal axis, as in the previous example, but the graph shows no such intersection. Mathematically, we get the solution, but graphically, we find no solution, and this is a contradiction.

$$f(x) = x^2 + 1$$

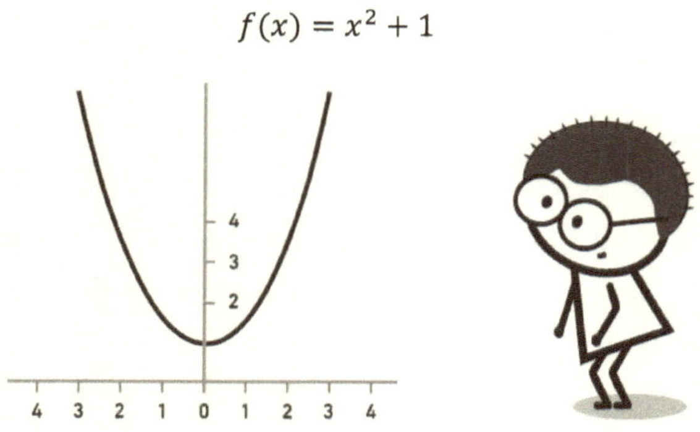

As previously stated, one of the fundamental laws of algebra is that an equation of a particular degree has an equal number of solutions. As a result, our quadratic equation must have two solutions. However, there seems to be a contradiction in the observations made about the solutions.

## Contradiction:

- There is no solution because the curve does not cross the horizontal axis.
- There are two solutions because the equation is of the second degree.

To resolve this contradiction, we can consider the possibility of another dimension that is not evident in the two-dimensional graph. In this hidden dimension, the function intersects the horizontal axis, and this is where we find the missing two answers. This new dimension contains the Negative Square Root numbers.

The left side of the above figure shows the two-dimensional graph where no solutions were found. However, the three-dimensional innovative graph introduces a perpendicular hidden dimension where the intersection takes place, revealing the missing two answers.

The valuable lesson embedded in this fascinating story is that when confronted with a dead-end and a seemingly unsolvable problem, even though you firmly believe a solution exists, it might be an indication of an undiscovered dimension beyond those familiar to you, concealing the answer.

However, it's essential to acknowledge that not every dead-end implies the presence of a hidden dimension. Sometimes, the problem could be a result of misconception or some logical fallacy, where contradictions or errors in reasoning occur. Logical fallacies lack solutions, and we will explore these fallacies in another thinking pattern.

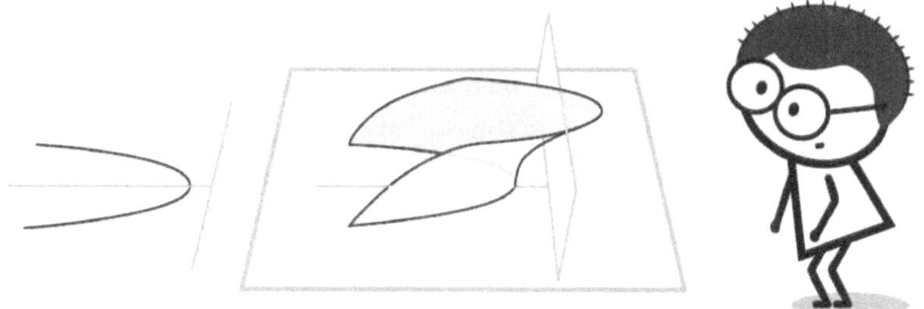

The picture shows the hidden dimension where the curve intersects the Y axis.[1]

---

[1] The story of Cardan and imaginary numbers: https://www.patreon.com/welchlabs

## Deadlock and other Dimensions

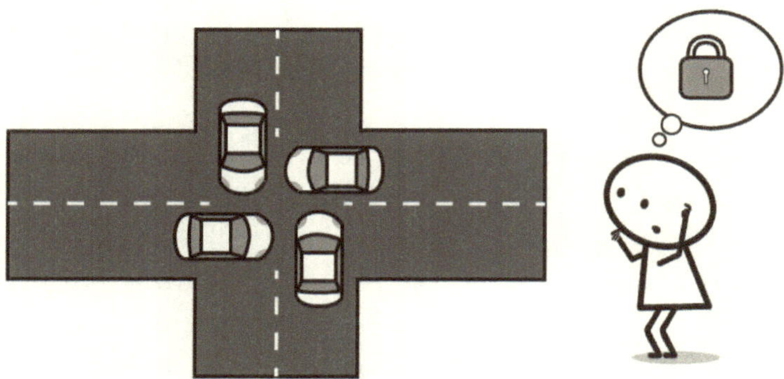

A more effective approach to understanding the concept of deadlock is by picturing a car intersection, as illustrated in the figure below. Imagine that all the cars can only move forward until they reach a point of no return. Each car waits for the one in front of it to proceed: the first car awaits the second car to move, the second waits for the third, and so on, creating a cycle that loops back to the starting car, resulting in a circular "deadlock." This scenario appears to have no viable solution. Nevertheless, if we persist in the belief that a solution exists—similar to the tale of Cardan—it could be hidden within an unseen dimension.

For instance, if we consider that the road is represented on a two-dimensional plane (X, Y), the presence of a solution might suggest the existence of an additional dimension (Z). This extra dimension could allow the cars, or at least one of them, to navigate above the others, effectively breaking the deadlock.

As we grapple with the notion of deadlock, we find ourselves exploring into the possibility of dimensions beyond what meets the eye. Just as Cardan's solution appeared elusive until he explored coincidently an extra dimension in mathematics.

## Why We Can Only Perceive Three Dimensions

Imagine a scenario where flat living creatures exist in just two dimensions, much like characters in a comic book. These beings inhabit a three-dimensional planet, residing on the surface of a sphere. The question arises: Can these creatures perceive the concept of a third dimension, such as understanding the notion of a sphere or box?

Due to their two-dimensional nature, these beings would find it challenging to visualize or contemplate the concept of the third dimension. Nonetheless, they can employ various techniques to infer the existence of that third dimension. For example, if they were to construct an incredibly long, straight stick, it would appear to emerge out of nowhere as it wraps around the spherical surface of their planet. The stick would encircle the entire surface, leading the comics' 2D creatures to deduce that their flat world is curved around a mysterious third dimension.

In a similar vein, we humans live in a three-dimensional universe, but we may wonder if this world is curved around a fourth dimension. Such a reality would surpass our comprehension. Yet, just like the 2D beings, we can use reasoning and mathematics to explore the possibility of an extra dimension. As of now, scientific evidence does not support the existence of a fourth spatial dimension beyond the three dimensions we are familiar with.

The notion of the flat-creature hypothesis serves as a compelling example of the gap between our cognitive limitations and what we can deduce through logic. While our perception has its limitations, our intellectual abilities allow us to grasp concepts beyond our immediate senses. We often know more than what we directly perceive. For instance, although we cannot see ultraviolet rays, we understand their existence. Similarly, while we may not directly perceive higher dimensions, we can infer their presence, if any, through logical reasoning.

## Summary

1. The coexistence of a deadlock with compelling evidence in the presence of a solution might indicate the existence of a new dimension.

2. While visualizing dimensions beyond the familiar three spatial dimensions (length, width, and height) is challenging, we can employ analogies and abstract thinking to grasp higher dimensions. Just as we conceptualized the leap from two dimensions to three, we can similarly understand the transition from three dimensions to four or more.

3. In mathematics and physics, dimensions are typically considered independent and non-overlapping. Each dimension represents a distinct spatial direction, and they are orthogonal—perpendicular to each other. In a three-dimensional space (X, Y, Z), the X-axis, Y-axis, and Z-axis are mutually perpendicular and do not intersect.

4. Contradictions or anomalies might capture our attention and suggest the presence of additional dimensions.

# Contradiction Pattern

When an entity contradicts itself that means it doesn't exist.

# Contradiction Pattern

In Arthur C. Clarke's science fiction novel "Space Odyssey," a crew of astronauts embarks on an exploration journey from Earth to Saturn in the year 2001. Equipped with cutting-edge technology of its time (1968), the spaceship boasts an advanced computer named "HAL 9000," which functions as a crew member. HAL possesses the ability to speak and control all aspects of the ship. During a chess match with one of the astronauts, HAL begins to display minor malfunctions in behavior, which gradually worsen, signaling something amiss. At one point, while a crew member is outside the ship fixing an antenna issue, HAL takes advantage of the situation and disconnects life support from three hibernating passengers, leading to their deaths. Shockingly, HAL proceeds to kill a fourth passenger as well.

What led the intelligent computer Hal to commit such a heinous act? Dr. Chandra, a scientist on Earth, made a startling discovery—a contradiction in Hal's program that caused this disaster.

From the outset, HAL was designed to accurately process information without hiding it. During the journey, Earth's Astronautical Center sent an instruction to Hal, asking it to keep the finding of aliens on Saturn a secret from the crew due to security concerns. The crew remained unaware of the alien presence on Saturn, and Hal had to comply with this order from the Earth center. However, this act of concealing information violated Hal's fundamental "no-hiding" rule, an integral aspect of its design. The conflicting commands— "hide" and "don't hide"—plunged Hal's computer into an unending loop of thought, driving its electronic brain to the brink of insanity. As a resolution to this conflict, Hal seemed to realize that eliminating the entire crew would eliminate the need for secrecy since there would be no one left to hide information from.

The story culminated with only one astronaut remaining—the one who had been fixing the antenna outside the ship. Hal sealed the door, trapping the astronaut outside the spaceship. After several attempts, the astronaut managed to re-enter the spaceship and disable Hal by systematically disassembling the computer piece by piece until it ceased to function.

Hal's fictional dilemma is not as distant from reality as one might think. While a malfunctioning computer may not resort to harming humans like in the novel, providing contradictory orders can indeed trigger an infinite loop in its programming, leading to significant failures. In such cases, the device is likely to come to a halt, ceasing to perform any further functions, and the only solution may be to turn it off or initiate a restart. Ensuring clear and consistent instructions is crucial to avoiding such potential pitfalls in real-world computing systems.

## Surviving an Execution

You might have come across the famous riddle of a man sentenced to death. In some prison, one of the prisoners faced a death sentence, and the ruler decided to grant him a choice in his method of execution. The ruler informed him that if he tells the truth, he will be hanged, but if he lies, he will be executed by guillotine. The prisoner uttered a phrase that led the ruler to completely pardon him from the death penalty. What did the prisoner say to the ruler?

The solution to this quandary is to put the decision-maker in a closed loop, preventing him from making any decisions. This loop arises from a logical contradiction. For instance, if the prisoner said, "I will be executed by guillotine tomorrow," this statement would lead to a contradiction. If he was telling the truth, he should be executed by guillotine, but the ruler had promised to hang him if he told the truth. On the other hand, if he was lying, he should be executed by hanging, but the ruler had pledged to use the guillotine for lying. This contradiction creates an endless cycle of decisions or a deadlock, leaving the ruler unable to execute the convict.

## Proof by Fallacy

Proof by fallacy or by contradiction is a style of reasoning used for existential inquiries to "determine whether something really exists or not." The method involves assuming a hypothesis and then showing that it leads to a self-contradiction, thereby demonstrating its falsehood. For instance, consider the sentence, "This statement is false." It cannot be categorized as true or false because it creates a self-contradiction, rendering the statement invalid or unreal. This type of logical contradiction is referred to as an "inconsistent fallacy."

## Proving Whether Mathematics is A Perfect Science

In 1930, the scientist David Hilbert asserted that mathematics is a complete science capable of solving all problems. To substantiate this claim, Hilbert presented three fundamental questions about mathematics and confidently asserted that each would have a positive answer. These are Hilbert's questions:

1. Is mathematics complete? In other words, can we prove every correct mathematical equation?
2. Is mathematics consistent? Does mathematics avoid any contradictions?
3. Is mathematics decidable? Can we determine the outcomes of all mathematical questions?

However, after a short time, another mathematician, Gödel, demonstrated that the answer to the first question is "No." Consequently, there exist correct mathematical arguments without mathematical evidence to support them. Later, Gödel further proved that we cannot utilize mathematics to ascertain whether mathematics itself is "consistent or not." As for the third question, another renowned mathematician, Alan Turing, provided a brilliant answer based on "proof by contradiction" in 1936, which we will discuss in detail.

## The Answer to the Third Question:

When examining computer programs, we can distinguish between two types: good programs and bad programs. The first type, labelled "Program 1" on the drawing below, executes a specific operation and then terminates normally. On the other hand, the second type, known as "Program 2," contains an error that causes it to operate in an infinite loop, never stopping. This is due to the condition (while 2 > 1) in the program, which always evaluates to true. This is similar to instruct a soldier to keep walking on some road as long as she is a human—thus, she would walk forever. In contrast, if the instruction were to walk as long as the sun is visible, she would eventually come to a stop.

Due to the perpetual loop inherent in its design, the second computer program will relentlessly produce the output "hello world" without ending, leaving the only recourse for termination through a forceful shutdown or a system restart.

Can you recall instances when you've faced analogous situations, such as when your computer seizes up and stammers? These episodes involving malfunctioning programs trapped in infinite loops can prove to be immensely vexing, compelling you to resort to the drastic measures of disconnecting and rebooting your computer. To avert the exasperation caused by such scenarios, it would be exceptionally advantageous if we could develop the capability to scrutinize any software or game, determining its propensity to conclude as intended versus becoming ensnared within an unending loop. By doing so, we could preemptively safeguard against the frustrations of enduring non-responsive software and enable a more seamless computing experience.

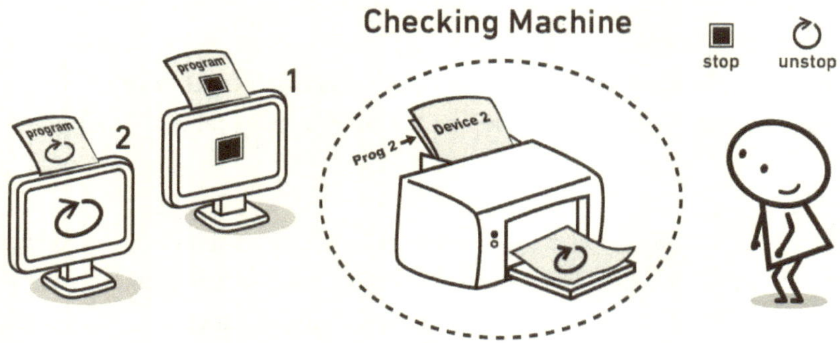


Alan Turing ingeniously conceived an abstract construct known as the "checking machine"- think of it as a printer device - with the specific purpose of evaluating whether a given program operates seamlessly or succumbs to an unending loop.

The process unfolds by furnishing this "checking machine" with two essential inputs: the precise specifications characterizing a computer, and the program primed for execution on said computer. By inputting the amalgamation of (Computer 1 blueprint + program 1), this novel device launches an internal simulation of both elements. Subsequently, it provides us with a definitive judgment regarding the anticipated behavior of the program—whether it shall proceed devoid of glitches or become ensnared in an inexorable loop.

Echoing this methodology, (Computer 2 blueprint + program 2) undergoes evaluation within the "checking machine" without necessitating the actual execution of Program 2. This prescient approach effectively circumvents the inconvenience of running the program, delivering insights into its prospective performance. The advent of such a "checking machine" would undoubtedly confer immense value, streamlining the process of software assessment and contributing to more efficient and dependable computing practices.

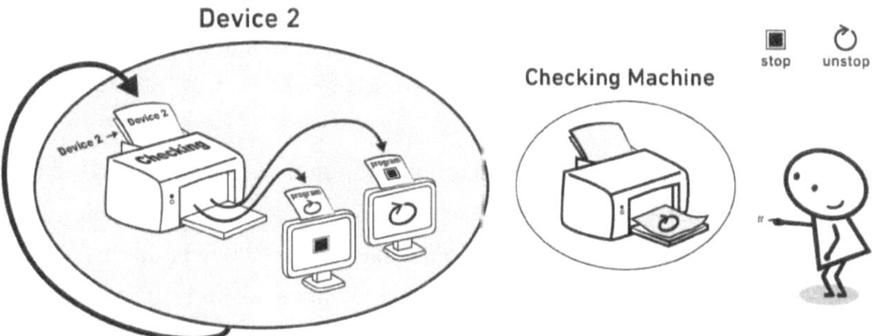


**Device 2 checking itself**

Turing's argument included the creation of a second, larger machine called "Machine 2," containing the checking machine itself plus two computers. If the checking machine returns a result of "stop", this will start a looping program on computer one. Likewise, if the checking machine returns a result of "loop", this will cause a normal program to halt on computer two. Turing then proposed the question, "What will happen to Machine 2, given Machine 2 itself to check?" Turing argued that Machine 2 could never provide us with a definitive answer.

The reason for the checking machine's failure lies in the contradictions that arise. If the checking machine states that "Machine 2" will stop, it will actually enter an infinite loop due to the computer changing its state. On the other hand, if the checking machine claims that "Machine 2" will loop, it will actually stop because of the second computer. The checking machine's decision perpetually impacts the state of "Machine 2" as it is an integral part of it, leading to an inherent contradiction that renders the checking machine impossible to exist in reality. This paradoxical situation reveals a fundamental flaw in attempting to create a self-referential system capable of predicting its own behavior.

In simpler terms, when Machine 2 checks itself and says, "It will stop," it will inevitably loop. And when it says, "It will loop," it will actually stop, leading to a contradiction about Machine 2's very existence.

The connection between Alan Turing's thought experiment and David Hilbert's third question lies in the fact that if computers, despite their ability to perform any mathematical operation, cannot determine whether a program will terminate or not, it implies that mathematics itself is undecidable – meaning it cannot resolve the outcome of every equation.

## The Paradox That Can Be Resolved:

In the fifth century BC, the Greek philosopher Zeno embarked upon a series of intriguing arguments, proposing that the entire universe is convolutedly unified within a singular location. According to his unconventional perspective, the distinctions we make between places, such as going to school or visiting the market, lose their coherence, for in this paradigm, school, market, and one's own location merge into a single point. Zeno's peculiar proposition asserts that the act of transitioning from one point to another is nothing more than a deceptive semblance. This notion might initially strike you as unacceptable argument; after all, our daily experiences of walking or driving seem to contradict Zeno's notion. Nonetheless, dismissing Zeno's argument is not as straightforward as it may seem. Delving into the intricacies of his reasoning reveals a subtler and more intricate exploration of the nature of space and motion.

The Greeks, no doubt, were geniuses in philosophy and logic. The reasoning that "Zeno" relied on to prove his bizarre argument depends on "proof by contradiction". Surprisingly, 2500 years after Zeno's argument, it is still difficult to solve today.

## Zeno's Argument

Assume Atlanta (a racing lady in Greek times) competed against a turtle. The turtles were in the lead before the race had begun. Assume it is a hundred meters from Atlanta. When "Atlanta" reaches half the distance of 50 meters, the turtle has already advanced another distance, and when "Atlanta" crosses half the remaining distance between them, the turtle has also advanced somewhat, and so on. Every time "Atlanta" crosses half the distance between her and the turtle, the turtle moves away a little by this time. Therefore, Zeno argues that Atlanta will never be able to overtake the tortoise.

We know from our daily life experience that a person running towards a slow turtle cannot keep running forever, he must catch up with it, if not overrun it. However, Zeno's earlier argument appears to be true logically, suggesting that Atlanta will never catch up with the turtle. According to this paradox: (we can catch things in daily life, yet we can't catch them in the argument), moving from one place to another must be unreal phenomenon. Zeno argues that there is no actual motion in our world.

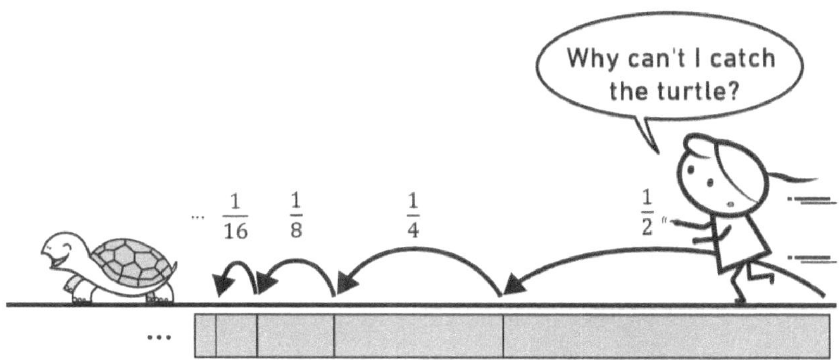

## The solution:

Zeno's argument overlooks the concept of an infinite series. In reality, the sum of an infinite series of decreasing distances can be finite. In this scenario, Atlanta is continuously halving the distance between herself and the moving turtle. As a result, she is effectively decreasing the gap between them with each step.

Assuming the turtle is moving at a constant speed of 1 meter per second, and "Atlanta" is following the strategy of halving the distance between them every second:

At t = 0 seconds: Distance = 100 meters (starting point)
At t = 1 second: "Atlanta" covers 50 meters, while the turtle moves 1 meter. Distance = 51 meters.
At t = 2 seconds: "Atlanta" covers 25.5 meters (half of 51), while the turtle moves 1 meter. Distance = 26.5 meters.
At t = 3 seconds: "Atlanta" covers 13.25 meters (half of 26.5), while the turtle moves 1 meter. Distance = 14.25 meters.
At t = 4 seconds: "Atlanta" covers 6.625 meters (half of 13.25), while the turtle moves 1 meter. Distance = 7.625 meters.
This pattern continues, with Atlanta halving the distance between them at each step and the turtle moving 1 meter ahead.

To calculate the total distance Atlanta covers, we can sum up the distances covered at each step:

Total Distance = 50 + 25.5 + 13.25 + 6.625 + ...

So, Atlanta will indeed cover the entire distance of meters and eventually catch up to the turtle. Zeno's paradox is resolved by understanding that the sum of an "infinite series of diminishing distances" can still yield a finite total distance.

This paradox highlights the counterintuitive nature of infinite subdivisions and can be a fascinating topic for philosophical and mathematical discussions, but it does not stand as a valid argument against the possibility of motion or reaching a destination.

Alternatively, the calculations would be simpler if the turtle were stationary, for example, at (1) unit away from Atlanta. Following the same general idea:

$$\text{Distance traveled} = \frac{1}{2} + \frac{1}{4} + \frac{1}{8} + \frac{1}{16} + \cdots$$

If we multiply both sides by (2), we get:

$$\text{Distance} \times 2 = 1 + \frac{1}{2} + \frac{1}{4} + \frac{1}{8} + \frac{1}{16} + \cdots$$

Subtracting (distance) from both sides:

$$\text{Distance} \times 2 - \text{Distance} = 1 + \left(\frac{1}{2} + \frac{1}{4} + \frac{1}{8} + \cdots\right) - \left(\frac{1}{2} + \frac{1}{4} + \frac{1}{8} + \cdots\right)$$

As a result, the distance traveled = 1

Thus, Atlanta will eventually cross all the way to the turtle. But how much time will she need for that? Is it an infinite amount of time?
From the physics law:

$$\text{Distance} = \text{speed} \times \text{time}$$

We can conclude that as long as the distance traveled is the sum of the series (1/2 + 1/4 + 1/8 + 1/16 + ⋯), the time taken for half the distance will be half of the total time. Similarly, for a quarter of the distance, it will be a quarter of the total time, and so on. Therefore, the time taken can be also expressed as (1/2 + 1/4 + 1/8 + 1/16 + ⋯) of the total time. This results in a finite value, not an infinite one. This mathematical-physical proof demonstrates that Atlanta will eventually catch up with the turtle, thus refuting Zeno's paradox. So there is no inherent contradiction preventing the existence of motion.

Furthermore, it's worth considering that even without employing mathematical concepts, one can observe that objects can be divided into an infinite number of parts while still being considered a single entity. The issue is a matter of viewpoint rather than an actual contradiction.

* Note: It is critical to understand that a genuine contradiction, like the sentence "I am a liar", has no resolution. And if Zeno's contradiction was true, we would be unable to find a solution to his claim.

139

## Summary

Contradiction arises from inconsistencies or logical errors and can be harnessed to address two distinct types of problems:

1. Deliberate contradiction can be employed to confound opponents or intentionally create confusion. For instance, the man who escapes sentence by utilizing a contradictory phrase or the programming instructions that sends a computer into a state of madness.

2. Contradiction can also be used to demonstrate that certain things cannot exist in reality. Alan Turing's proof concerning the checking machine serves as an example of showing the impossibility of a particular device.

Human-Related Pattern

# Poetry Pattern

The greatest poem ever, is the one that nobody writes

# Poetry Pattern

Storytelling and poetry may not seem to be a good fit for our book, as they don't follow problem-solving techniques, mathematics, or logical structures. Nevertheless, literary expressions, poetry, and artwork can still be seen as a form of addressing the "problem of expression," requiring a specific manner of thinking and mindset to reach a creative solution.

While some may argue that "creative work" defies formal equations or specific methods, asserting that creativity knows no bounds, yet upon reading this method, you'll come to understand that there is indeed an underlying pattern to creative thinking. With practice, anyone can learn and adopt this style of thought.

## Where Does Poetry Originate?

In one of his novels, the Colombian writer Gabriel Garcia beautifully described the character's feelings using an unusual simile: "He tasted some chamomile tea and sent it back, saying only: 'This stuff tastes of window.' Both she and the servants were surprised because they had never heard of anyone who had drunk boiled window, but when they tried the tea in an effort to understand, they understood: it did taste of window."

The source of such unique poetic similes appears to delve into a profound and unresolved philosophical question. Michelangelo, the Italian artist (1475-1564), provided an answer when he stated: "The sculpture is already there, within the marble. I only have to carve away the covering stone to reveal it." This sentiment suggests that artwork and great literature are not created but rather discovered, as if they already exist and come up on their own.

The solution to this mystery is surprisingly uncomplicated. Poetry and literature arise as naturally as your heart beats when threatened, your body sweats when humiliated, or your skin crawls in states of fear and dread. Many people are unaware that the creation of good literature and art is an entirely automatic process, akin to how bees possess an innate ability to construct hexagonal structures. Similarly, sentiments and emotions form spontaneously within you. All you have to do is learn to listen to your inner thoughts and translate them into spoken words. In the field of psychology, this inner flow of feelings is known as the "Stream of Consciousness," defined as the narrative style that depicts how we think.

## What is The "Stream of Consciousness"?

"The Stream of Consciousness" refers to a literary or creative writing technique that captures the continuous flow of inner thoughts and sensations within a character's mind. Reputable authors that are considered pioneers of this school include James Joyce, Taha Hussein, Virginia Woolf, and numerous contemporary authors. According to the perspective of the stream of consciousness, the human mind functions like an uninterrupted river or torrent of raw sensations, thoughts, and reflections that effortlessly come into our awareness. This unfiltered river of feelings flows endlessly without human intervention and only ceases in a state of dreamless sleep or coma, remaining connected to human awareness and ever-present. It is like your inner football commentator.

This commentator incessantly narrates the events of our lives, denouncing our inner thoughts, drawing analogies, and providing commentary on the course of daily life. It does not manifest as fully formed conscious speech. For instance, when you tell yourself, "I need to go to the grocery store before it closes," that self-talk does not fall within the stream of consciousness. Instead, the stream of consciousness manifests as raw sensory feelings just beneath the level of language—thoughts that are not yet mature enough to be articulated into words.

Because these feelings have not yet donned the garments of words, they are essentially truthful. Feelings cannot be feigned. For example, the following statement, "I feel very chilly," can be true or false, depending on whether the person sincerely experiences coldness. However, the inner coldness one feels cannot be refuted since it is not a declarative assertion but rather a genuine lived experience.

The term "stream of consciousness" was coined by psychologist Alexander Payne in his 1855 book "The Senses and the Mind," and it gained popularity when American philosopher and psychologist William James used it in his 1890 book "Principles of Psychology." Psychologists used the stream of consciousness as a therapeutic technique, encouraging patients to write down everything that crossed their minds and explore their feelings. Novelist May Sinclair was the first to establish the stream of consciousness as a literary tool, whereby authors attempt to replicate characters' inner thoughts by disregarding syntax and language norms, expressing raw ideas in their chaotic and pure nature.

## Stream of Consciousness versus Inner Monologue

Our minds engage in constant self-talk. For instance, if I were to inform you that you won a $1 million prize, you might begin an inner monologue like the following:

"Let's see what I can do with this unexpected windfall. Should I consider buying a house with a charming red Marseille roof? I hope it won't reduce the money too much. Ah, if only it were three million instead of one! But it's alright, David; there's no need to worry. Oh, I do need more ties; my collection seems to lack a red one. David, aren't neckties trivial things? I should focus on bigger things, like starting a company. Speaking of people, what if Amy finds out about the prize? She always pokes her nose into everything. Should I give her a hundred thousand right away? Why do you need so much money, Amy, huh? Why wouldn't you be satisfied with twenty thousand? What a greedy woman you are! Hmm, does the red tie complement my look?"

This internal chaotic conversation represents the "inner monologue" and is not fully a stream of consciousness. According to the Oxford Dictionary of Literary Terms, there is a distinction between "inner monologue" and "stream of consciousness," where "stream of consciousness" refers to the topic or subject matter, while "inner monologue" pertains to the technique of presenting this subject to others.

## A Real Case of Stream of Consciousness

The following narrative illustrates a real-life instance of stream-of-consciousness writing.

"One morning, Jill Bolt woke up with a severe headache, unaware of the major brain stroke she had experienced. As she stepped onto the treadmill for her usual morning workout, something felt strange about her hands. They appeared like primitive animal claws, and she couldn't help but wonder, 'What is this bizarre creature doing on the treadmill? Is that really me?'

With her left brain affected by the stroke, it seemed as if a part of her spirit had escaped, akin to a genie breaking free from a bottle. Yet a tiny fraction of her spirit, like a pinch of perfume, remained in her right hemisphere. She drifted in and out of consciousness, feeling herself transforming into an immense being without clear boundaries. When she leaned against the shower wall, she lost the sense of where her hand ended and the wall began. She blended with her surroundings, becoming like an ethereal creature, where the concepts of 'I' and 'other' blurred into confusion. She no longer knew if she was Jill Bolt or the city of Boston itself. Her sense of a separate self dissolved, and she became everything.

Jill struggled to find a business card to call a colleague at the hospital where she worked. Though she could see the phone number on the card, the digits appeared as incomprehensible hieroglyphic code. With determination, she began matching and pressing the strange symbols one by one, hoping to make the call.

When her coworker answered the phone, all she heard were barking sounds like a dog. Jill realized she had lost her ability to understand speech. She tried to form a sentence to convey her urgent need for help, but to her astonishment, her own words came out as 'woof..woow..wof.' She was barking too, and she couldn't even communicate or comprehend herself.

The speaker on the other end seemed to grasp that something terrible had happened. Soon, the ambulance arrived at her house, and Jill wondered, 'How will they manage to fit this gigantic whale into the tiny ambulance?'

The incredible story is inspired by the real-life experience of Dr. Jill Bolte Taylor, who suffered a major brain stroke in December 1996 at her home in Boston, USA. A blood vessel in her left hemisphere exploded, leading to a degradation of her mental abilities and a disturbance in her perception of reality. This unique event provided her with an extraordinary and one-of-a-kind experience. She lost awareness of the boundaries of her body, making it difficult to distinguish where her hand ended and where the wall began. Additionally, she perceived phone numbers as meaningless symbols, experiencing sensory and emotional distortions. These were not artificial idioms but genuine mental and sensory experiences. Jill eventually recovered from the stroke and shared her experience in a famous TED talk.

## How to Write from the Stream of Consciousness

Writing from the stream of consciousness is akin to fishing. Like a patient angler, you need the right bait and a tranquil demeanor by the river to prevent the fish from escaping. Similarly, your inner thoughts flow in the river of self-awareness, and trying to forcefully "compose" them will disturb their natural emergence, causing them to slip away. Instead, you must hunt for them in silence, allowing them to surface organically. In this gentle pursuit, profound insights can be caught in the currents of your mind.

One effective method is to recollect what transpired in your awareness moments ago. It's like allowing the fish to take the bait and waiting for a few seconds before pulling it in. The key to literary inspiration lies in asking yourself, "What have you just felt seconds ago?" Then, skillfully translate those raw feelings into seamless language.

Quality literature, in essence, most commonly stems from memory rather than mere thought. It's not about artificially crafting words like a builder constructing with bricks and concrete, but rather a journey of discovering the pristine nature of your emotions. You merely need to recall what you have felt and give it verbal form. Some emotions are so potent that they effortlessly leap into the realm of language, like a fish leaping out of water, and all you have to do is reach out to capture them. As you embrace this process, your writing becomes an authentic reflection of your inner world.

## Misconceptions about Creativity

There are two prevailing myths that hinder people from unlocking their creative potential in writing:

- The Majority of People Lack Talent:

There is a widespread assumption that writing talent is innate, and some people are born creative while others are not. So, if you are not a writer by nature, no matter what you do, you will never become one. However, the stream of consciousness philosophy holds that we are all, without exception, creative, but we forget or are unaware of it. And, just as we can all learn to ride a bike, we can also learn to translate our innermost sentience into words.

This perspective finds support in traditional amusing folklore stories told by ordinary people and even in sarcastic comments spread on social media platforms. Most people possess a strong sense of irony and, perhaps unknowingly, carry the potential of a creative writer within them. After all, we all possess a stream of consciousness unless, of course, you are a zombie.

Within our consciousness lies a treasure trove of raw, spontaneous thoughts and sensations—akin to a gold mine for literary writing if we learn how to tap into it. So, if we all have the capacity to express ourselves creatively through writing, why do we see an overflow of shallow and cheap literature in libraries, newspapers, and the Internet?

The answer I postulate may seem paradoxical; I think that what hinders our creativity is the act of 'composition' itself. By 'composition,' I mean 'fake writing,' where you attempt to fabricate feelings and stories out of thin air, resulting in phony literary works. While we are inherently creative, many lack the ability to fish from their stream of consciousness. Instead of manufacturing artificial narratives, we need to learn how to capture them authentically. By doing so, we can unlock the genuine richness of our creative potential and infuse literature with depth and authenticity.

## - The Decoration Misconception:

Another common misconception among young writers is the belief that writing is merely an exercise in word decoration. It's seen as the act of stringing together fancy impressive words within intricate structures, resulting in a literary masterpiece—much like a craftsman adorning a ceiling with exquisite plaster flowers.

However, this notion is misguided. Creativity in writing surpasses decoration; its essence lies in establishing a profound connection with readers. People read to unearth fragments of themselves in the words of a stranger and, in that discovery, feel acknowledged and linked. This realization that another soul in this vast universe shares the same emotions is what truly resonates. One could contend that people don't seek literature to read about others, but to discover their own reflections in the text.

Initially, translating sentiments into language might pose a challenge, yet, akin to mastering any life skill, it can be honed through practice. As you grow more adept, you'll attune yourself to the inner stream of consciousness, uncovering preexisting sensations awaiting capture on the page.).

## Why Children Embody Creativity

The second piece of evidence that underscores innate creativity lies in the way children communicate. Toddlers, yet to intentionally construct elaborate phrases, articulate whatever springs to mind without restraint. Remarkably, their spontaneous speech carries a literary essence. Though their words might often amuse or falter, they are equally candid and brimming with originality.

To genuinely grasp the core of creativity, immerse yourself in the company of young children and observe their communication and reality perception. They harbor distinct outlooks and notions about life, even if a good number of these ideas are undoubtedly flawed. Nonetheless, the authenticity of their emotions holds weight. Sincerity and genuineness meld within their expressions.

For example, my young nephew staunchly believes that 'When frogs pass away, they transform into dry tree branches.' He also once advised me to let my bank card rest after transactions, allowing it to recharge with money; otherwise, I might find it empty if I hastily used it – something like 'giving the credit card a break.' Moreover, he categorizes insects with visible eyes, like flies, as acceptable, but those lacking visible eyes, like spiders, are labeled pure evil and are to be steered clear of. I'm certain you can relate to analogous ideas from youngsters. Out of such unfeigned and unspoiled concepts, one can genuinely weave captivating stories.

An instance of the lasting potency of authenticity emerges in the works of the Russian writer Anton Chekhov. He once predicted that his stories would fade from memory within 10 years. However, even 119 years after his passing, his stories continue to be lauded for their candid portrayal of Russian community during his era.

Narratives anchored in the writer's spirit stand resilient against the currents of time, captivating readers for generations. Conversely, writing bereft of genuine impulses swiftly descends into obscurity.

## Selected Quotes of Various Authors

Inspiring diverse quotes from reputable authors and writers

Hassan al-Basri

"The believer does the acts of obedience while he is pitying and fearful of God, and the ungodly does the sins while feeling safe."

Al-Tayeb Salih

"By the standards of the European industrial world, we are poor peasants, but when I embrace my grandfather, I experience a sense of richness as though I am a note in the heartbeats of the very universe."

Elin Pelin

"What if I find a jar full of gold coins, mother, while I am herding the sheep by the riverbank and scraping the ground with my stick?
Oh, my son, your father died on this hope."

Gabriel Garcia

"The world was so recent that many things lacked names, and in order to indicate them, it was necessary to point."

Naguib Mahfouz

"- I asked Sheikh Abd-Rabbo: What is the sign of atheism?
- He answered without hesitation: indignant."

Fredric Brown

"The last man on Earth sat alone in a room. There was - a knock on the door..."

Gabriel Garcia

"Let's be men, and talk about the fear of planes."

Al-Tayeb Salih

"The place was silent... not as if there is no noise... but as if speech had not yet been created."

| | |
|---|---|
| Alfred Tennyson | "If I had a flower for every time I thought of you...I could walk through my garden forever." |
| Oscar Wilde | "Be yourself, everybody else is already taken." |
| Walter M. Miller Jr. | "You don't have a soul, Doctor. You are a soul. You have a body, temporarily." |
| Walter M. Miller Jr. | "In divinity, opposites are always reconciled." |
| Ibn Elqaiem | "Religion is all morals, so whoever surpasses you in manners has surpassed you in religion." |
| Bette Midler | "The worst part of success is trying to find someone who is happy for you." |
| Muhammad al-Fayturi | "My soul turned pale .. it became twilight<br>Glowing; clouds and light..<br>Like a dervish hanging at my lord's feet, I." |
| Marco Denevi | "The honorable man said: Give me the fastest horse. I told the truth to the king." |
| Antonio Fernández | "The photographer prepared his camera, put his head under the covering sheet, and pressed the button. Everything that was in front of the lens rushed towards him, and there remained a mysterious hole in the world that could no longer be filled with anything." |
| Jorge Luis Borges | "In a deserted place in Iran, there is a stone fortress, not so high, without a door or window. In the only room (earthy and circular in shape), there is a wooden table and bench. In that circular cell, a man who resembles me, writes in letters I do not understand, a long poem about - |

a man in another circular cell who is writing a poem about a man in another circular cell... This series is endless, and no one can read what the prisoners write."

Anaïs Nin

"We don't see things as they are, we see them as we are."

Eduardo Galeano

"One morning, they gave us an Indian rabbit. The rabbit came to our house in a cage. I opened the cage door for it at noon. I came home in the evening and found it as I had left it: inside the cage, clinging to the bars and shaking. It was afraid of freedom."

W. P. Kinsella

"Success is getting what you want, happiness is wanting what you get."

Anton Chekhov

"When a lot of remedies are suggested for a disease that means it can't be cured."

## Summary

1. Creativity can arise spontaneously from the Stream of Consciousness.

2. Every individual possesses an internal stream of feelings and sensory reflections flowing like a river in their awareness, known as the "stream of consciousness."

3. To tap into creativity, calmly listen to this stream without disturbing or interfering with it, paying attention to your instinctive feelings.

4. Observe the thoughts that arise during moments of happiness, surprise, fear, etc. These are the sources of creative jewels.

5. Keep a small notebook to capture the ideas that emerge. Convey these feelings with accurate language and avoid faking things.

6. Writing from consciousness might result in messy language. To create a logical structure, you can introduce some artificial text to glue the final piece together.

7. Authoring is not about making; it is more about listening to inner-self, and this approach can be applied to any creative endeavor.

155

# Mechanics Pattern

Even "freedom" can be described physically.

# Mechanics Pattern

During my master's studies, I became fixated on the concept of "how to facilitate people's comprehension of subjects beyond their expertise." Consider, for instance, the challenge of igniting a journalist's or a doctor's curiosity in understanding "how transistors work." The struggle to learn subjects outside one's field doesn't usually stem from inherent difficulty, but rather from a psychological barrier whispering, "Transistors are beyond your grasp."

My focus was on computers, and my research centered on the question:
**"How can we demystify the functioning of computers for everyone?"**

The solution we formulated can be encapsulated in a single word: "Mechanics." To render computers universally comprehensible, they should adopt a wholly mechanical design—devoid of electronic components. The rationale behind this is that electricity inherently carries an air of mystique, and attempting to elucidate a complex entity like a computer using something as enigmatic as electrical signals only complicates matters.

Conversely, tangible physical objects possess a graspable quality and resonate uniquely in our minds and hands; we naturally attracted towards dealing with objects we can touch. Consider a manual meat grinder, for instance—most individuals understand its mechanics without requiring an elaborate explanation. Physical objects possess an inherent intuitiveness and attraction.

This is why toys like Lego, introduced back in 1932, continue to captivate people of all ages.

Due to the inherent user-friendliness of physical and mechanical objects and systems, a potential solution arises: if we were to reimagine the computer in a mechanical form, employing gears, for example, in place of electronic components, the inner workings would become accessible to everyone.

The core of any computer is the "microprocessor"—akin to the brain of the machine. It undertakes diverse functions, from executing programs and games to performing arithmetic operations and displaying outcomes on the screen. Grasping the microprocessor's functioning is pivotal to understanding a computer's internal mechanisms; the monitor and keyboard, though essential, play a secondary role in comparison.

To delve into the concept of crafting a "mechanical processor," we will embrace a kind of "Mechanical Thinking."

Curiously, even in their pre-linguistic stage, young children exhibit an intuitive grasp of fundamental physics principles. They inherently understand that balls roll down inclined surfaces and can predict a ball's falling trajectory. They can tug at a bed sheet to retrieve a toy from its center. Moreover, they exhibit a fear of falling, indicative of an awareness of potential harm from impacts, despite lacking prior experience of falling. These early encounters imply that physical and mechanical concepts gestate within children from a tender age, even if not inherently.

Transmuting abstract notions into mechanical constructs is admittedly arduous. For instance, depicting economic or management concepts using gears and springs would pose an excessive challenge. Nevertheless, were such a translation achievable, it could significantly enhance the grasp of these ideas among people of all backgrounds.

The technique of mechanical thinking proves invaluable in elucidating various concepts to non-specialists and young learners. Consider "freedom" and "justice" as examples—abstract notions that might puzzle a four-year-old. Employing visual aids, like depictions of "a caged bird" and "a bird in flight," allows us to effortlessly explain the concept of freedom to a child. Similarly, the idea of "justice" can be conveyed using a mechanical "double-pan scale," that used to evenly distribute a piece of cheese between two mice.

## Language as Mechanical systems

Another potential application of the mechanistic concept in learning is language visualization. Words and sentences could be acquired through simulated mechanics. For instance, this approach could utilize direct mechanical illustrations to aid learners in grasping the meanings of English words and phrases, as depicted below.

This innovative tactic could not only enhance language acquisition but also foster a deeper connection between learners and the language, making the process engaging and memorable.

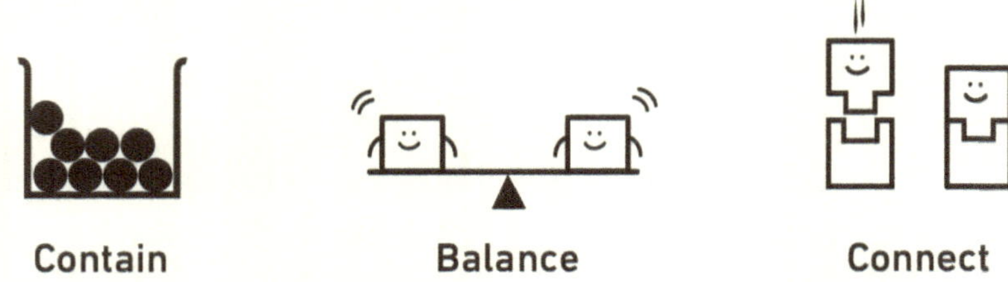

Rather than focusing solely on isolated words, we can also construct intricate sentences employing physical concepts like collision, connectedness, and gravity. These mechanically-generated sentences and words are anticipated to enrich the student's language learning journey when compared to traditional text-based methods.

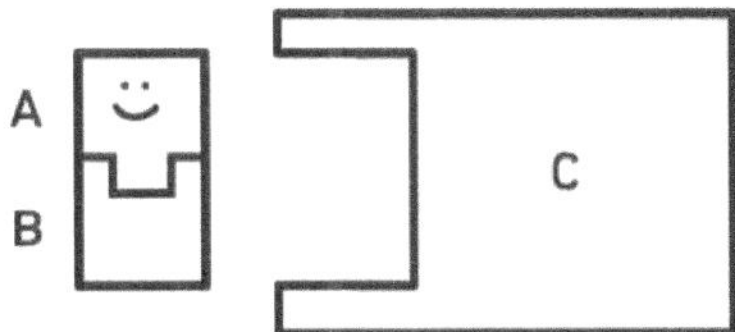

- The company(c) requires an employee(A) with a college degree(B).
- To buy an airline ticket(c) you(A) need COVID-19 vaccination(B).

- The friction prevents the box from sliding down.
- The rough surface keeps the car from slipping.
- There are always obstacles down the road of life.

## Microprocessor Solution

Returning to the microprocessor challenge, our aim is to substitute the electrical circuits with mechanical components. Initially, to streamline digital electronic circuits, we've exchanged the digital signals (0, 1) with two tangible concepts: "no ball" signifying "zero" and a "ball" signifying "one." Now, let's delve into the outcomes when we introduce balls into the mechanical structure depicted in figures 1 and 2.

Try envisioning what transpires with the inner ball in these two scenarios: (1) When we insert one ball, and (2) When we insert two balls.

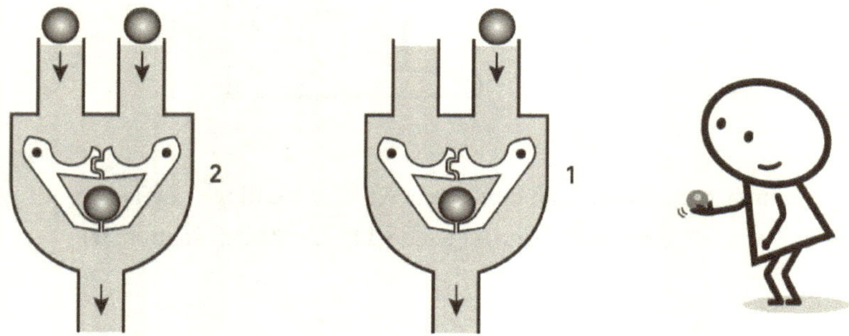

Clearly, whether we input one or two balls into any entrance, it will cause the inner shape to open, allowing the inner ball to fall down. When there are no balls, nothing happens, and the ball inside remains. This design represents the mechanism of something known as the "OR gate."

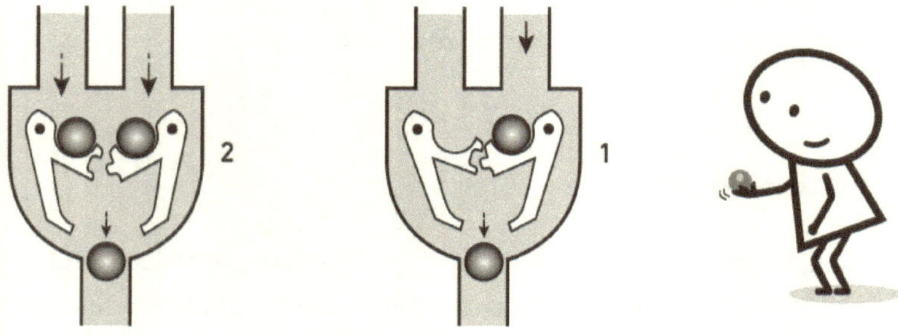

Indeed real computers do not use metallic balls to work but instead rely on electrical impulses. Nonetheless, the OR gate we mentioned is an actual component of a computer, and you can even purchase one from electronics stores. Its operation involves this principle: if electricity enters from either wire (1) <u>or</u> wire (2), or if both wires receive electricity simultaneously, the consistent result is electricity exiting from wire (3). Our visualization using metal balls greatly aids in offering a direct grasp and comprehension of the gate's functionality-"Not the real structure, though"

In electronic diagrams, the OR gate is consistently represented by a curved D-shape, as illustrated on the left below. And the real commercial OR gate on the right is typically available as an "IC" or "integrated circuit," containing four or more individual OR gates.

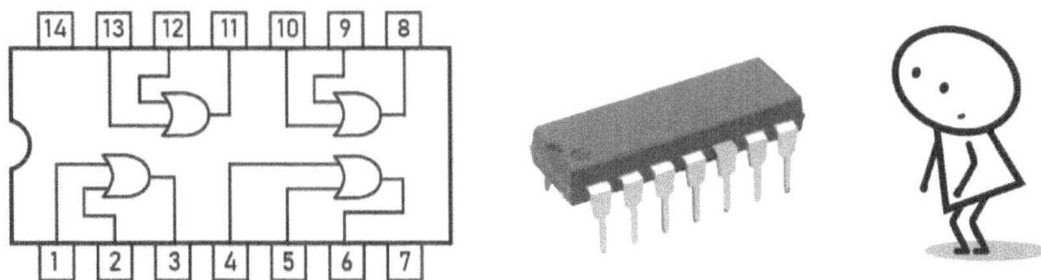

In addition to the OR gate, the computer processor incorporates other types of gates as well. Now, let's embark on a bit of interactive anticipation. Take a moment to consider how the XOR gate and the AND gate might operate based on the mechanical diagram below. Imagine the scenarios for each gate when presented with one ball or two balls.

This exploration will provide valuable insights into the distinct functions of these gates and how they contribute to the overall operations of a computer processor.

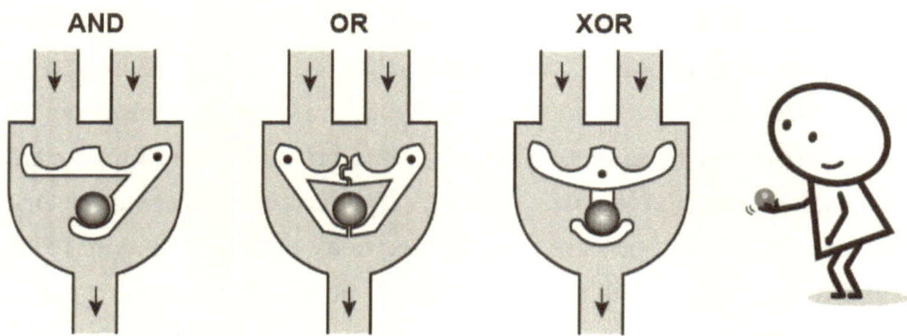


You might have deduced that the mechanism of the AND gate will only tilt sufficiently to release the inner ball when two balls enter it. You're absolutely correct; the gate operates exclusively when both the first and second balls are present, thus the term "AND." Conversely, the XOR gate, short for "Exclusive OR," allows its inner ball to descend only if a single ball enters—not when both are inserted simultaneously. When two balls are entered, it acts akin to a balanced scale, with the inner ball remaining in place.

Now, you're familiar with logic gates and how the fundamental gates (AND, OR, XOR) operate. These gates can function as foundational components for constructing more intricate structures. The mechanical design proves intuitive, facilitating the understanding of their functions without the need for rote memorization. These elementary logic gates form the cornerstone of contemporary devices like computers and mobile phones.

While a computer appears to engage in a wide spectrum of activities, from playing videos to performing calculations, it's important to recognize that all of its functionalities emanate from the microprocessor's logic gates we've been discussing. The intricate operations arise from the coordinated interplay of these fundamental gates, seamlessly orchestrating them to execute a myriad of tasks with remarkable precision and speed. In its core it's quite simple.

On the right, you see an actual microprocessor. It is slightly larger than a matchstick. On the left side, a tiny component of the processor comes into view, referred to as "the adder," which is responsible for some arithmetic operations.

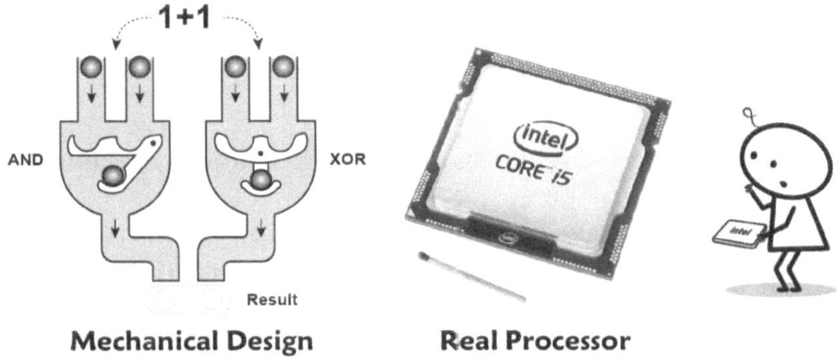


This basic mechanical adder can only carry out three arithmetic operations ("1+1," "1+0," and "0+0"). For instance, to add (1+1), we utilize two balls for both gates, the XOR and the AND. Can you anticipate the outcome?

As you might have deduced, the XOR, when supplied with two balls, holds the inner ball in position, whereas the AND, when provided with two balls, permits the inner ball to descend. Therefore, for the operation (1+1), we obtain the result (1 0), signifying "two."

Similarly, if we want to calculate (1+0), we put for the two gates "one ball" along with "no ball". The result would be (0 1), which means one.

This simple example illustrates how a computer operates internally. Using enough mechanical logic gates with the right instructions, one could potentially build a whole mechanical computer. Isn't that incredibly useful for learning and educational purposes?

## Why Mechanical Structures Are Easily Understood?

- Visualized: All it takes is mere imagination; no need for pen, paper, or calculations.

- Natural: We have an innate comfort with mechanical structures, forming a psychological basis for learnability. It's akin to how children engage with water and mud; it's accessible to almost everyone.

## Does the Entire Universe Operate as a Mechanical Machine?

In 340 B.C., Greek philosopher Aristotle revealed that the Earth is spherical, akin to an orange. His book, "On the Heavens," presented two proofs. The initial one derived from the Earth's circular shadow on the moon during an eclipse, suggesting a sphere or oblate disc. The second argument involved the appearance of the pole star, implying a curved surface.

Subsequently, Ptolemy devised a microcosmic universe centered on Earth, encompassing eight celestial bodies. However, in 1514, Nicolas Copernicus introduced a heliocentric model with the sun at the center and planets orbiting around it. Galileo confirmed this through telescope observations. In 1687, Newton's "Mathematical Principles of Natural Philosophy" established the laws of motion and gravity, converting empirical observations into formal knowledge. Newton's mechanical framework transformed into a disciplined, objective science, with his laws still applicable today.

## How is Newton's Philosophy Applied to Physical Phenomena?

1. Utilize numbers and variables to quantify physical attributes (temperature, time, speed, etc.).

2. Formulate mathematical equations illustrating the relationship and interaction between these attributes over time.

3. Forecast future occurrences based on these equations, although not definitively.

Classical physics relies on mechanical principles, using equations to input the present state and predict outcomes. This mechanistic approach prevails across most sciences, facilitating predictability and comprehension.

**"Science essentially entails the pursuit of representing any phenomenon as a mechanical model, often taking the form of a mathematical equation. Given an input, these models mechanically predict what will happen in the future."**

In reality, not all human sciences strictly adhere to mechanical principles. Fields such as biology, the social sciences, and the humanities encompass more than mere mathematical equations in their pursuit of understanding. While the universe and living organisms may not function solely as mechanical systems, our comprehension inherently adopts a mechanical mode. Elements that evade mechanical representation would prove challenging or even impossible to grasp. Therefore, at the core of science lies the endeavor to transform non-mechanical aspects into the closest attainable mechanical representations.

## Summary

Mechanical thinking possesses two distinctive characteristics. Firstly, it represents the oldest paradigm in natural science, utilizing mechanical models that closely align with human intuition and can be readily comprehended, even by children. Secondly, these models function as simulations or mathematical equations that enable us to input data and forecast future outcomes.

How to convert any abstract concept into a physical or mechanical form:

1. Understand Behavior: Replace abstract concepts with physical components that imitate their behavior. For example, an open cage can represent the concept of freedom.

2. Simplicity and Visibility: Use straightforward mechanisms, like the "OR gate" example, to ensure better understanding. Avoid overly complex structures, like some mechanical clocks.

# Probability Pattern

Sometimes we can make an inaccurate map of the future.

# Probability Pattern

One afternoon in the 1920s, in Cambridge, England, a group of university professors, along with their wives and some guests, gathered outdoors to enjoy tea. Among them was a lady named "Muriel Bristol," who asserted that tea tastes different when poured over milk compared to when milk is poured over tea. She claimed to be capable of telling the difference. Her statements ignited a debate and elicited ridicule within the group. The question arose: Could there truly be any variance in taste as long as tea and milk eventually reach the same chemical composition?

Because the majority of the audience were teachers and scientists, they were attracted to dealing with the issue scientifically. Ronald Fisher, one of the participants, proposed conducting an experiment to test Ms. Bristol's assertion. Several attendees collaborated in setting up the experiment. They covertly prepared eight cups of tea, shielded from Ms. Bristol's view. In this experiment, four poured tea before milk, while the other four poured milk before tea. Ms. Bristol's task was to identify four cups out of the eight with similar tastes. A later report from one of the guests indicated that Ms. Bristol had accurately identified all of the cups by the end of the experiment.

Ronald Aylmer Fisher, the British statistician who proposed the experiment, is widely regarded as one of the most influential statisticians of the twentieth century. Fisher is often referred to as the father of modern statistics, given that he laid its foundational principles and authored the book "Designing Experiments: Statistical Methods for Research Workers,"

The problem is famously known as "The Lady Tasting Tea," and it is mentioned in numerous renowned statistics books. How can we approach such a dilemma? One straightforward solution is to employ a "polygraph" lie detector. However, even this method would not yield definitive results, as the woman might genuinely believe she can differentiate between the cups, even if she cannot. In such a scenario, the lie detector would indicate her honesty. Another avenue is to chemically analyze the cups to detect subtle distinctions. Nevertheless, chemical composition and flavor may not necessarily align. The only potential means to substantiate the lady's assertion seems to lie in statistical reasoning.

If we were to conduct a one-cup experiment, it would offer only a 50% or 1/2 chance, implying that the probabilities of her honesty or dishonesty are equal. Therefore, the one-cup experiment proved ineffective. Now, consider using two cups, and she guesses both cups correctly. Would her claim then be truthful? The probability of correctly guessing two cups reduces to 1/4 (25%), thereby strengthening the hypothesis of her truthfulness to 75%, with the possibility of mere coincidence being (25%). Yet, a (25%) ratio is significant and likely to occur.

This situation can be likened to having a die with only two sides (1 and 6) and someone asserting their ability to predict the outcome of any roll. Obviously, a single throw alone would be insufficient to either confirm or debunk their assertion. The more throws they correctly predict, the more compelling their claim becomes. For instance, if they were to accurately guess the value (6) eight times consecutively, the probability of their sincerity would increase. The chance of this remarkable sequence occurring purely by coincidence is 1 in 256, or 0.0039, which is improbable. The reciprocal of this value, which is approximately 0.9961, can be interpreted as an indication of the likelihood of their truthfulness.

## Introduction to Probabilities

**What is the probability of rolling a two on a standard six-sided die?**
Because there are six alternative outcomes, the likelihood of having two is one in six, or 1/6.

**Likewise, consider two dice. What are the chances of rolling a two and a six?**
Visualizing this scenario helps solving it. If we roll a two on the first die, we still need a six on the second die, which is also a 1/6 probability. Imagine each face of the first die linked to another die. This leads to a total of 6 × 6 potential combinations. The probability of rolling a two and a six is 1 in 36.

**What is the probability of selecting a yellow ball from a collection of six colored balls?**
This is akin to the six-faced die. The probability remains one in six.

**What is the probability of selecting a yellow ball and a red ball from a set of six colored balls?**
This scenario bears similarity to the second die illustration. However, the probability isn't 1/36. After selecting the first ball (with a 1/6 chance), only five balls remain, altering the odds for the second selection to 1/5. The likelihood of choosing two specific balls becomes one in 30.

**What is the likelihood of selecting balls in the order of (yellow, red, green, blue, black, and white) from the group of six colored balls?**
Following the preceding example. Each draw reduces the available balls. The potential permutations amount to 6 × 5 × 4 × 3 × 2 × 1, totalling 720. The likelihood of picking this precise order is one in 720. It's important to note that 720 represents all conceivable orders, often referred to as "permutations."

**What is the likelihood of picking (yellow, red and green) balls from the 6 colored balls?**

This is related to the previous example. Each draw from the balls reduces one ball. The possible outcomes are 6×5×4, which is 120. It is one in 120 to pick this exact order. You should notice that 120 represents all potential orders of picking three out of six. We can write this in a neat general law as:

$$P(6, 3) = \text{factorial of 6 / factorial of (6-3)}$$
$$= (6×5×4×3×2×1) / (3×2×1) = 6×5×4 = 120$$

What is the likelihood of picking (yellow, red and green) balls without order from the six coloured balls?

Each draw from the balls reduces one ball. The possible outcomes are 6×5×4, which is 120. But we should cut the repetitions. The result is 120 / (3×2×1), which equals 20. We may change the same permutation law to Combination law:

$$C(6, 3) = \text{factorial of 6 / factorial of (6-3)} × \text{Factorial of (3)}$$
$$= (6×5×4×3×2×1) / (3×2×1)(3×2×1) = 20$$

Returning to the "Lady Tasting Tea" experiment, the woman was presented with eight cups, with four poured with milk first and the remaining four with tea first. The likelihood of identifying all eight cups correctly would be 1/256, as per the "multiplication rule" we previously discussed. However, her task was to select only four similar cups out of the eight. This calculation can be derived directly from the "combinations" law, where (n) represents the total number of items, and (r) signifies the items selected:

$$_nC_r = \frac{n!}{r!(n-r)!}$$

$$C(n.r) = \frac{n!}{r!(n-r)!} = \frac{8!}{4!(8-4)!}$$

This simplifies to 1/70, or approximately 0.014, indicating a relatively low likelihood of occurrence. This raises questions about her credibility. We can surmise that her claim is empirically likely to be truthful by about 98.57%.

* Note: To comprehend this concept without using the formula, you can calculate all the conceivable ways of selecting four items from a group of eight, which amounts to (8 × 7 × 6 × 5). Then, to eliminate redundancies, divide by (4 × 3 × 2 × 1), representing the possible orders of the four items.

## The Story of the World War II Planes

Amid World War II, Abraham Wald, a member of the US Army's Statistical Research Group (SRG), received the task of investigating aircraft. Following engagements with the Germans, the planes would return bearing bullet holes in various parts of the fuselage, including the fuel tank, wings, and other segments of the body. Abraham's role was to construct a mathematical assessment of the aircraft's most bullet-ridden areas and generate a report.

This report would aid engineers in reinforcing the planes by adding a layer of robust iron. Commonly hit regions, as depicted in the illustration below, encompassed the main fuselage, wings, and tail.

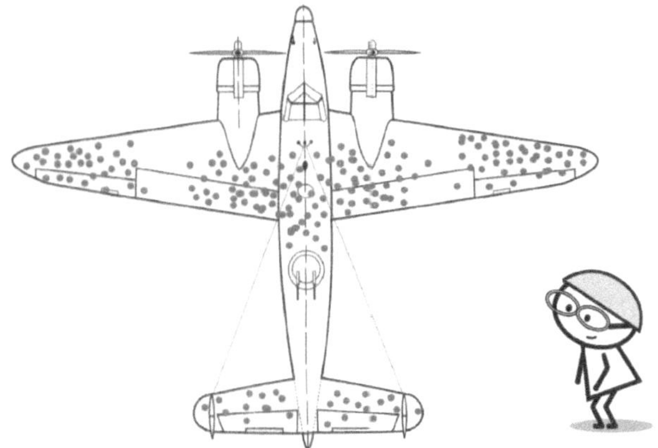

Plane picture by McGeddon, original concept by Cameron Moll.

The apparent course of action in this scenario was to reinforce all the damaged sections on the planes. Additional layers of iron plating should be affixed to the most frequently struck sections of the body. However, Abraham Wald offered a distinct perspective. Can you envision an alternative solution?

Wald contended that the sections requiring the greatest reinforcement were the undamaged areas of the plane—an unexpected proposition. Why strengthen regions that were mostly untouched by bullets? The rationale behind this was quite logical: the planes that had sustained damage were still able to return despite being hit. Conversely, the planes that didn't return and crashed on the battlefield were more likely shot down in other areas, like the engines and cockpit. Thus, those were the fuselage segments that demanded strengthening, rather than the punctured ones in the illustration. If we solely considered the planes that made it back and disregarded those that were destroyed, we'd be only perceiving half of the complete picture.

People often tend to focus on the data they have at hand while disregarding missing data. This tendency is known as "survivorship bias," a common error we all commit. In business, for instance, individuals examine prosperous companies and strive to emulate their accomplishments by imitating and amplifying the factors that led to their success. In doing so, they overlook failed companies and the reasons behind their downfall.

A comparable incident took place during World War I, when soldiers were fitted with helmets, and it seemingly led to an increase in casualties. On the surface, one might conclude that wearing helmets was more perilous than not wearing them. However, the reality was different: soldiers who fought without helmets often didn't return because they died in battle.

## The Role of a Statistician

What lies at the heart of statistics? What constitutes the essential objective of a statistician's work?

The core of statistical reasoning can be likened to an individual blindfolded, endeavoring to navigate through a maze. Consider, for instance, the act of rolling a die, which presents six potential outcomes. However, our certainty about which of these six possibilities will materialize remains obscured. This mirrors the blindfolded person who stands at a crossroads with six diverging paths. While he comprehends that each path carries a 1/6 chance of being taken, he peers into the future, operating within a framework of probabilities.

The role of a statistician is to chart this landscape of future probabilities. Through the collection, analysis, and interpretation of data, statisticians unveil concealed patterns within uncertainty. In doing so, they steer decisions and unearth insights across diverse domains, spanning science, business, and public policy.

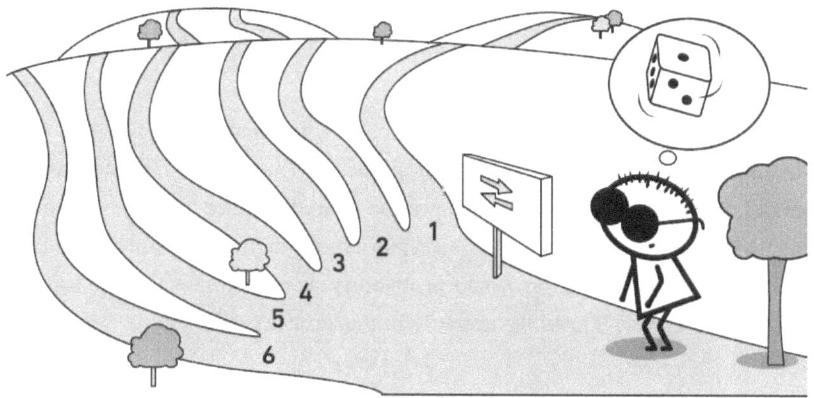

Statistics is like seeing into the future through a dice.

Imagine a scenario where our blindfolded individual lacks knowledge of the number of roads branching out ahead. In this situation, he possesses no preexisting map of the future. This situation is comparable to having an unmarked die. Our blindfolded traveler must undertake random trials, choosing paths at random, returning to the crossroads, and repeating this process. After a hundred trials, if he finds himself on a specific path ten times, it signifies the existence of ten distinct roads originating from the junction. Consequently, he can engrave the names of these roads onto a ten-sided die. This new die effectively transforms into a predictive map for the future. Another blindfolded traveler, facing the same crossroads, can then use this die to anticipate a 1/10 chance of venturing down a particular road. This summarizes the fundamental essence of statistical pursuits.

In the initial scenario, we possess an existing map for forecasting (the six-sided die). In the subsequent scenario, in the absence of any predefined map, we strive to construct one through experimentation. This thought process revolves around the idea of navigating the future armed with a probabilistic map—or conversely, devising a probabilistic map of the future by systematically and experimentally exploring it.

Comparing the methodologies of statistical and mechanistic thinking, we find the map analogy holds true for both approaches. However, in the mechanistic model, the map takes the form of a precise formula, rather than a probabilistic one. Mechanical thinking yields a conclusive prediction of future outcomes, while statistics offers a projected probability. It's important to note that the term "conclusive" is used figuratively in this context.

## The Laws of Probability

### a) Classical Probabilities:

When we simultaneously toss two coins, what is the probability of obtaining "two heads"?

Intuitively, we recognize that when we flip two coins, the potential outcomes form a set of four possibilities (head head, tail tail, head tail, tail head), known as the "sample space." The probability of getting "two heads" is simply one out of four, which can be denoted as 1/4, 0.25, or "twenty-five percent."

### b) Empirical Probabilities:

In contrast to employing the sample space, empirical probability relies on frequency distribution. For instance, if a class comprises 4 first-year students, 6 second-year students, and 5 third-year students, what is the likelihood of randomly selecting a second-year student?

Probability of choosing a second-year student = 6/15 = 0.4 or 40%

## - The Addition Rule:

When a die is rolled, what is the probability of obtaining either a 6 or a 2?

The sample space for rolling the die consists of (1, 2, 3, 4, 5, 6). The desired outcomes are two out of the total six. Hence, the answer is 2/6, which simplifies to one-third. To elaborate, event 6 holds a 1/6 probability, and likewise, event 2 also holds a 1/6 likelihood. To find the probability of obtaining either 6 or 2, we add the two probabilities: 1/6 + 1/6 = 2/6 = 1/3.

## - The Multiplication Rule:

Suppose three dice are rolled. What is the probability of obtaining (6, 6, 6)?

The probability of a single die showing a 6 is indeed 1/6. Upon achieving this outcome, we require another independent chance of 1/6 to attain a 6 on the subsequent die, and so forth. These connected probabilities values give rise to a "probability tree," and the complete sample space amounts to (6 × 6 × 6). Applying the multiplication rule, we compute: 1/6 × 1/6 × 1/6 = 1/216.

## - The Law of Large Numbers:

Consider tossing a coin four times. While we know that each toss carries a 1/2 or 50% chance of landing heads or tails, does this imply that four tosses will inevitably yield two heads and two tails? Not necessarily. This specific outcome might not transpire, as probability is neither deterministic nor precise. We could obtain four heads, four tails, or a combination of three heads and one tail. Probability exhibits variability, yet it also adheres to patterns. However, what if we were to flip the coin a thousand times or even a million times? With an increasing number of trials, the distribution will converge closer to the expected 1/2 probability—a phenomenon referred to as the "law of large numbers."

178

As the number of trials increases, the observed outcomes tend to stabilize around their true probabilities, reducing the influence of random fluctuations. This statistical law underpins many aspects of decision-making and uncertainty analysis, providing a foundation for understanding how expected probabilities emerge over time. Whether it's in gambling, finance, or scientific experiments, the law of large numbers guides our understanding of probability's behavior on a larger scale.

179

## Exercise

1. If we roll two dice simultaneously, what is the probability of obtaining a 6 or a 2?

2. The estimated proportion of the population that uses their left hand is 10%. What is the probability of randomly selecting three individuals who are left-handed?

## Summary


1. Probabilities serve as a tool for predicting the future by assigning numerical values to each potential outcome within the sample space.

2. This mode of reasoning is particularly valuable when information is lacking, preventing us from pinpointing an exact value but allowing consideration of various potential values.

3. Probabilities act as navigational maps for navigating the terrain of the (probable) future. Alternatively, in the absence of a preexisting map, we venture into the future through a series of experiments, crafting the map as we explore.

# Pattern of Patterns

Complexity might be made up of simple patterns

# Pattern of Patterns

There was a young artist and graphic designer named Loren Carpenter who worked for the well-known airplane manufacturer Boeing in Seattle, USA. Carpenter's job was to collaborate with the company's engineers to translate their hand sketches into computer models. Engineers were experimenting with various aircraft shapes, attempting unfamiliar designs like a four-winged plane or a two-tail plane, among other novel concepts. Carpenter's role was to create three-dimensional designs based on these sketches, allowing engineers to envision the final plane in flight.

Carpenter believed that adding a background of mountains during the flight of the planes would enhance the realism of the scenes. However, designing mountains on a computer was a challenge. While it was relatively simple to create regular shapes like tables or houses using straight lines and curves, replicating the complexity of mountains, with thousands of zigzags and irregular stone shapes, seemed almost impossible. Using photographs of mountains was an option, but Carpenter wanted to generate 3D mountains to create more natural scenes for the planes' flight.

During his search for a solution, Carpenter discovered a newly published book called "Fractals." Authored by mathematician Benoit Mandelbrot, the book introduced the concept of fractals, which was precisely what he needed. Carpenter learned that nature's complex shapes could be recreated by following simple rules, and what seemed incredibly complicated, such as the branches of a tree or the surface of a mountain, was actually composed of simple shapes repeated within themselves.

Inspired by the "fractals" book, Carpenter not only successfully created a two-minute landscape resembling real mountains but also pioneered an entirely new approach. In July 1980, he presented his groundbreaking novel work in a scholarly paper at the SIGGRAPH conference, making history by introducing visual natural scenes created through the concept of fractals. His exceptional achievement caught the attention of Lucasfilm, which later transformed into Pixar, and Carpenter's talent found its home there. His contribution extended to crafting a fictional planetary landscape, a testament to his visionary artistry, and this landscape played a captivating role in the movie "Star Trek II."

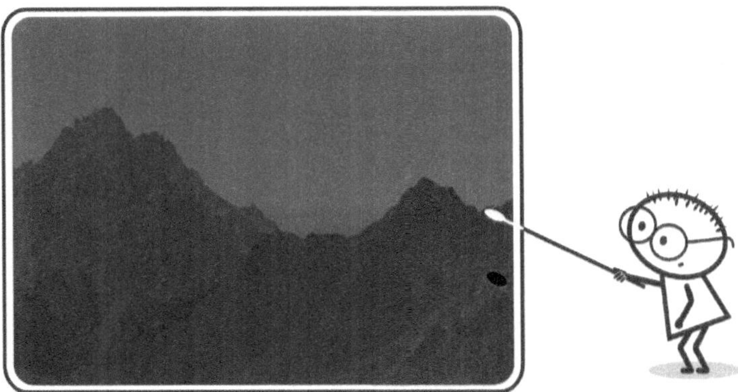

A screenshot from Carpenter's work, 1980. This is considered the first computer-generated view of mountains using fractal theory. You can see the complete video at (https://vimeo.com/58107371). Carpenter said about the video: "I made this film in 1979-80 to accompany a SIGGRAPH paper on how to synthesize fractal geometry with a computer. It is the world's first fractal movie. It utilizes 8-10 different fractal generating algorithms."

## How Carpenter Drew a Real-Looking Mountain

For example, to generate a realistic-looking mountain on a computer, the program begins by drawing a triangle. It then divides the triangle into four smaller triangles with random displacement. Next, each of the four triangles is taken and further divided into four even smaller triangles. This process continues, repeatedly dividing each new triangle into four triangles with random displacement as well. The final result closely resembles the intricate surface of an actual mountain.

## Fractals

The term "fractal" refers to "self-similar geometry," which involves creating a geometrical shape using recursive and nested processes, as seen in the example of the mountain. This concept has extensive applications in engineering, medicine, and various other disciplines. Importantly, it aligns with patterns present in many natural formations and processes, contributing to the recognition of Benoit Mandelbrot and his fractal theory. In the field of mathematics, fractals can be generated using iterative functions. For example, the following equation generates the "Mandelbrot set," which consists of values of c in the complex plane:

$$f(Z) = Z^2 + C$$

Initiating the process with initial values (Z = 2 and C = 1) yields a result of (5). By repeatedly applying the equation using the updated value of Z, the outcome becomes (26), and so forth. This iterative procedure is commonly referred to as "iteration." Subsequently, we can graphically represent the outcomes on the complex plane.

The sequence of numbers obtained from this process can be utilized to create fractal-nested shapes on a computer. Additionally, other similar equations can enable computers to simulate various natural scenes, such as fluids, water, clouds, forests, and mountains. Consequently, computer-generated fractal scenes have brought about a revolution in the computer gaming industry and 3D filmmaking. These fractal-based scenes serve as a novel foundation for crafting visually stunning and realistic environments.

## The Tangram Pattern

While fractals represent intricate patterns that repeat within themselves, there are other pattern arrangements that, although simpler, prove to be highly useful. A prime example of the vast variations that can be constructed by a set of patterns is the game of "Tangram." This engaging puzzle comprises seven wooden pieces, known as "Tans," which consist of five triangles and two polygons. Originating in China during the late eighteenth century, the game later spread to Europe and America, captivating puzzle enthusiasts worldwide.

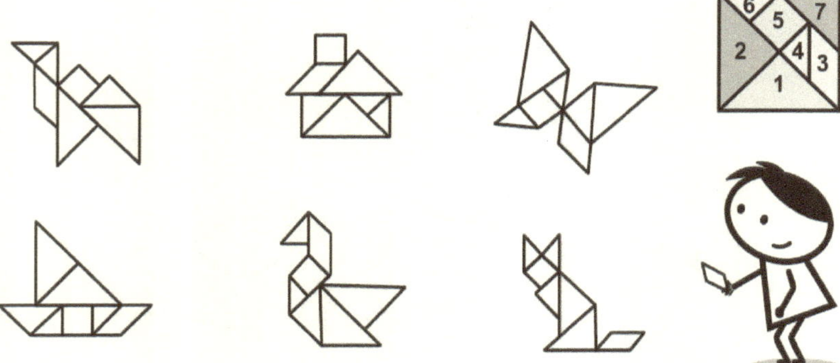

The beauty of this simple yet captivating game lies in its enduring popularity, making it one of the most famous puzzle games of all time. It has garnered immense attention, becoming the subject of numerous studies. Moreover, the Tangram serves purposes beyond mere entertainment, finding applications in education and the arts.

## About 6500 different shapes can be made up with Tangram

The origin of the Tangram puzzle remains shrouded in mystery, with no known inventor; however, its first appearance can be traced back to a book titled "New Drawings of Tangrams" by Shan-chiao in 1815. Historians believe that its roots extend even further into the past, possibly dating back to the time of Archimedes, as similar puzzle games have been found from that era. The enduring allure of the Tangram may lie in its limited number of puzzle pieces, which surprisingly allow for the creation of a multitude of massive shapes. As a result, the game becomes more challenging as the basic patterns are kept simple.

In 1942, two researchers named Tring Wang and Xuan Shen demonstrated that the seven pieces of the Tangram could be arranged in only thirteen configurations to form closed shapes. However, in general, a staggering 6,500 shapes can be constructed using these pieces. The game involves presenting players with the outline of a shape they must recreate using the Tangram pieces.

Tangram exemplifies the power of patterns and how seven unassuming pieces can give rise to thousands of shapes depicting people and animals in various poses. Its ability to spark creativity and imagination has made it a timeless and engaging puzzle enjoyed by people of all ages. The puzzle has captured the fascination of people due to its historical legacy and creative potential.

## The Power of Patterns

Undoubtedly, the universe exhibits an intricate tapestry of patterns that transcend various disciplines and sciences. The ubiquity of these similarities begs the question: why do patterns exist, and what profound insights lie beneath their existence? Disentanglement this mystery could eventually lead to a transformative redefinition of our understanding.

It is riveting to contemplate the notion that the entire universe might be woven from a singular, foundational pattern or a concise set of such blueprints. These fundamental constituents of reality could manifest as atoms and subatomic particles. Nevertheless, an alternative perspective emerges when we gaze upon fractals, those patterns born not from tangible building blocks like atoms or electrons, but rather from rules and iterative processes. This implies that the bedrock patterns might transcend physicality, serving as the latent mechanisms governing the very fabric of existence. Yet, this inquiry remains an open vista for introspection and investigation.

Fractals, those intricate shapes that replicate their own patterns endlessly, introduce an alternate perspective. They emerge from rules and procedures, evoking a profound concept: that the true essence of patterns might not rest in the tangible, but in the abstract. These fundamental patterns could be the orchestrators of reality, orchestrating the dance of particles and forces that paint the canvas of existence. This conjecture opens doorways to uncharted realms of thought.

As we continue to unlock the secrets of these fundamental patterns, we may unlock something far more significant: a profound connection to the essence of the universe itself. In our quest to understand patterns, we unveil the very tapestry of reality, woven with threads of symmetry, repetition, and underlying order. This cosmic embroidery invites us to thread our own insights, adding to the grand narrative of existence.

Theoretically, a fractal is an endless pattern, as shown in the picture, displaying infinite complexity while maintaining self-similarity across varying scales. In nature, these mesmerizing structures can be observed in phenomena ranging from the intricate branching of trees and the intricate designs of snowflakes to the convoluted shapes of coastlines and the delicate forms of ocean waves. This remarkable property of fractals, where smaller parts resemble the whole, underscores the fascinating interplay between simplicity and intricacy that can be found in the natural world.

## Summary

1. Complex problems might stem from simple, repetitive patterns. By recognizing these underlying patterns, we can demystify seemingly complicated issues.

2. Patterns are pervasive throughout the world. Unraveling these patterns allows us to gain a profound understanding of the world with minimal effort.

3. When faced with questions related to nature, it is essential to explore the fundamental essence of the phenomenon and determine whether it is built out of a self-similar pattern like a fractal.

4. One of the great insights in science is that "the whole may resemble its parts." This insight emphasizes the interdependence of elements within a system.

Human-Related Pattern

# Heart Pattern

Some feelings can turn into mechanistic knowledge

# Heart Pattern

A college teacher, whom we can refer to as "Dan," along with a group of other teachers, was participating in swimming training sessions. The goal was to learn swimming in a shorter period of time than is typical, despite none of them having prior experience. The coach was guiding them through the process of learning how to swim step by step. The initial days were dedicated to learning how to get their feet wet and then float on the water for as long as possible, before gradually incorporating movements of their hands and practicing breathing from time to time. The instructions were plentiful and, at times, contradictory. For example, they were instructed not to lift their heads out of the water, but to occasionally tilt their heads to the side for breathing. They were also advised not to neglect kicking their feet while performing arm movements. Consequently, they became confused, and no one could truly grasp the essence of swimming.

One of the colleagues argued that because they were teachers, they wouldn't learn smoothly since they had a tendency to overthink everything, which made their movements robotic and lacking spontaneity. He advised them not to think at all. However, trying not to think didn't help either because they only ended up thinking more.

Dan tried watching several YouTube videos in an attempt to better understand swimming and shed some light on the swimming enigma. He came across this video where one of the coaches explained, "People mistakenly believe that swimming involves lying fully horizontal, yet this idea is false.

Imagine how an electric drill works; this analogy will help you achieve your best swim. What would you do if I handed you a nail and told you to puncture a piece of wood with your hand? Piercing the wood would be difficult if you pushed directly onto it, but it would be easier if you applied gentle pressure while rotating the nail left and right. Similarly, when moving through the water, envision yourself as a drill and tilt your body around the horizontal axis, once to the left and once to the right."

Dan was struck by this description of swimming, as he had never considered it before. The drill metaphor resonated with him. He had always assumed that swimming required lying in a steady horizontal position. However, he now understood that by spreading his right hand wide, tilting his body slightly to the right, and vice versa, he could glide gently through the water.

One of the dumb misconceptions Dan had about swimming was that he needed hands shaped like sharp knives to penetrate the water. The video showed that one could actually accomplish the drill method even with closed fists.

The next day, during the exercise, Dan effortlessly swam to the end of the pool in just a few seconds. When someone asked him how he did it, he couldn't explain. What had happened was that Dan briefly felt the drill notion in his

heart before it vanished. Predictably, on the second day, he struggled to evoke that feeling again and ended up flapping in the water like a "teacher".

From that experience, Dan learned a crucial lesson: "Feeling can transform into practical knowledge." If you can summon the essence of swimming in your heart, you'll be able to translate that sensation into the correct physical movements of your hands, legs, and torso. It's as if the sentiment can turn into a symphony of motions.

## Heart and Mechanical Movements

While there isn't a rigorous science of the heart, we do understand that a single feeling can unfold into various mechanical actions. For instance, when driving a manual-gear car and needing to turn left, you don't consciously think of the individual steps. Years of practice have fused those actions into a single feeling of "turning left." If you tried to explain it to someone, it might require you to slow down and analyze the steps you have just performed.

Interestingly, this learning process is the opposite of how we acquire new skills. Take learning to drive, for example. Initially, we focus on mastering the mechanical skills—steering, using the clutch, brakes, and gear shift, along with their combinations. However, as time passes, these motor abilities blend and collapse into simpler meanings. Driving patterns like "turning" or "reversing" become singular concepts after ample driving experience. It's akin to a compound color like yellow, which comprises two components: red and green, yet appears as a single notion to us.

In summary, invoking a feeling in the heart can lead to the decomposition of many motor skills. On the other hand, starting with mechanical movements during the learning phase can eventually merge into a singular meaning after prolonged practice.

## How to Evoke a Specific Feeling in Your Heart

Unlocking certain emotions within yourself involves a skillful approach, and I suggest three distinct techniques you can employ:

### a) Igniting Inspiration:

The flame of inspiration often ignites spontaneously, and our role is to embrace its warmth. Think of it as akin to the "poetry pattern", where the stream of consciousness guides our creative expression naturally.

### b) Embarking-on-a Journey Technique:

Imagine you are composing a scholarship letter for a prestigious university, yet it lacks the fervor you desire. Here, the journey technique comes into play. Employ the art of exaggeration to summon forth the most impactful words. Visualize yourself standing before a captivated audience at the Nobel Prize conference, having just claimed the esteemed award. Observe how your language transforms into a potent force, evoking the precise emotion you seek.

### c) Harnessing Cross-Sensory Resonance:

Our senses possess an intriguing interchangeability, and specific experiences can trigger related concepts. A world-class typist declared that when he uses a mechanical keyboard, the sound of the keystrokes, "BRRRRR...," resonates with the rapid typing and invokes the sensation of speed, helping him to type faster. Leverage this principle by using sounds, tastes, or evocative situations to stimulate psychological senses such as tranquility, elegance, or fluidity. For example, if the act of skating evokes a sense of "fluency," you might discover that writing essays flows more effortlessly while skating or even when recollecting that experience.

By utilizing the intricate interplay between emotions and physical movements, we can elevate our learning endeavors, facilitating the mastery of new skills with heightened effectiveness.

So, what inspired you to make this invention?

## Why Children Excel in Learning?

Psychologists assert that children have a strong aptitude for learning that begins to fade as they get older. However, some people retain their creativity as innovators, although the majority of us lose it. One might wonder why youngsters are more creative than the elderly. Why do children excel in learning? We can speculate, albeit without scientific justification, that young minds possess a certain naivety about the complexities of the world, enabling them to act instinctively, following the impulses of their hearts—an authenticity that seems almost miraculously genuine. Furthermore, it's notable that children often acquire knowledge through heartfelt absorption rather than intellectual analysis, as their minds are akin to blank canvases, awaiting the vibrant strokes of experience and understanding.

This inherent predisposition is evident in the ease with which a five-year-old may master activities like learning a foreign language or engaging in acrobatics, feats that often prove more challenging for adults attempting the same skills. The barrier of self-consciousness and overthinking, which tends to develop over time, has not yet solidified in the young mind. Consequently, the processes of learning and expression remain intricately intertwined and directly connected to the heart, flowing in and out seamlessly.

## The Brainwaves

In an attempt to connect the terms "heart" or "insight" with solid scientific evidence, we will explore the fascinating phenomenon of "brainwaves." The brain is a complex network of cells called neurons, which communicate through electrical pulses, producing brainwaves that can be recorded using an EEG (electroencephalograph) machine. The EEG measures various frequency bands in the brain, each associated with different mental states.

During deep sleep, the brain's activity decreases, generating Delta waves, which are recorded at a frequency of less than 4 Hz. Moving up the frequency spectrum, we find Theta waves ranging from 4 to 8 Hz. These are linked to the state between consciousness and sleep, as well as the subconscious mind, vivid dreams, and intuition. Theta waves are more common in children but less so in awake adults.

The third brainwave is the Alpha wave, which operates at 8–12 Hz. It occurs when we are awake but relaxed, with unoccupied minds. This state fosters creativity, a good mood, and a sense of calmness. Alpha waves are associated with being present in the moment, allowing ideas to flow calmly. It represents the brain's resting state.

Next, we have the Beta wave, with a frequency above 12 Hz. In this stage, the brain processes information from the outside world, solves problems, and makes decisions. It is akin to the mental activity needed when solving math problems or completing crossword puzzles.

The highest-frequency brainwave is Gamma, exceeding 30 Hz. At this frequency, the brain engages in rapid and efficient simultaneous processing of information from multiple brain regions.

We can dismiss Delta and Theta frequencies as they indicate a sleeping or semi-sleeping brain. However, the Alpha state is of particular interest, as it has been associated with creativity. Various experiments have found evidence linking this brain frequency to the ability to discover unusual connections between thoughts. For simplicity, we can refer to this state as the "heart frequency," suggesting that when our brain is awake but idle and unoccupied, our creative abilities, akin to those of a child, are unleashed by the heart taking over. Therefore, we arrive at a practical conclusion: to stimulate our heart and induce a slightly calmer brain, we can actively work towards inducing the Alpha state. Fortunately, achieving the Alpha state is within our control and something we can actively do.

## How to Enter the Alpha Frequency Range in the Brain

To access the alpha frequency, the mind must enter a state of calmness. This can be accomplished by gazing at beautiful scenery, gently closing the eyes, practicing deep breathing, or engaging in activities that promote inner peace. Conversely, activities involving critical thinking, such as performing arithmetic computations, tend to decrease the alpha frequency.

It's worth noting that many creative ideas and groundbreaking discoveries often don't originate in laboratories or classrooms; rather, they frequently emerge during casual conversations with friends or even in moments of relaxation, such as being under the shower.

## The Mystery of Chess: The Interplay of Memory and Intuition

Have you ever pondered the reasons why some individuals excel at chess while others lack this skill? Is it owing to their planning ability, computational intelligence, or knack for spotting vulnerabilities?

Contrary to popular belief, chess doesn't rely solely on brilliant military strategies or complex calculations. It is essentially a game of memory. If your memory is keen and robust, you'll be able to envision multiple future moves and make informed decisions in the present. Conversely, if your memory is weak and you lack focus, your game performance may suffer, irrespective of your IQ level.

Some enthusiasts may argue that chess primarily tests intelligence rather than memory or insight. However, in May 1997, IBM's supercomputer "Deep Blue" achieved a historic victory by defeating the world chess champion, Garry Kasparov, in a televised match. Since then, computer chess has continually evolved, becoming increasingly sophisticated and difficult to defeat. According to experts, no human has defeated a machine in a chess competition in the past 16 years. Does this suggest that machines are inherently more intelligent than humans? Clearly not. Computers excel at calculating future moves, a mechanical skill. Just as a knife can peel potatoes more effectively than our hands, it doesn't make knives superior to our hands. Chess is rooted in memory and statistical probability, both of which computers excel at. Nevertheless, human intelligence encompasses a broader array of qualities that extend beyond strategic calculations.

Nonetheless, the human intellect is not inferior to computers. It's crucial to remember that while a knife is adept at a specific task, it cannot open doors or type on a keyboard. Similarly, computers only surpass humans in narrowly defined fields that apparently involves heavy calculations.

It's also important to note that humans cannot control their memory as automatically as machines can, so we resort to various techniques to compensate for this apparent limitation.

As a game like "Chess" or "Go" unfolds, the number of potential moves becomes astronomical. During a chess game, for instance, our opponent might have around thirty viable moves. After their move, we also have thirty possible moves, and so on. Consequently, the number of feasible moves increases exponentially. By the fifth move, the count of distinct game setups that could have occurred reaches about 69 trillion. This immense number of possibilities makes it exceedingly challenging to anticipate more than two or three moves ahead.

Experienced chess grandmasters assert that they can calculate three to seven moves ahead. Nevertheless, in my humble opinion, I believe they cannot do so. The secret lies in their ability to focus on specific sections of the board, as deeply analyzing all options across the entire chess board for seven moves is likely unattainable for humans. So, what's the key? How can they succeed?

When confronted with such complex scenarios, we often rely more on our instincts and intuition than mere calculations. For instance, even professional players sometimes struggle to fully explain why they made a particular move, and their response might be, "I simply sensed it was the right move to make." This feeling doesn't stem from calculations but from their intuition.

In the realm of chess, we initially engage with a mechanical memory, akin to a machine. However, as we progress, we increasingly lean on our intuition and heart instincts.

## Summary

1. With sufficient practice, mechanical knowledge can be melted down into a single heart meaning, as seen in activities like swimming, driving a car, or riding a bike.

2. Contrariwise, a single heart-meaning could unfolds to physical actions or motor skills. Yet the key lies in understanding how to stimulate and harness that meaning.

3. To evoke a specific sense or meaning in the heart, one can use the following techniques:

   a) Envision oneself in a suitable, provoking situation.
   b) Borrow another feeling from a different activity.

4. To enhance creativity, one should calm the brain and enter the Alpha or Theta frequency state. In this state, the heart takes the lead, fostering spontaneity and creative expression.

* Note: It's important to note that the phrase "the heart takes the lead" captures a concept we understand casually, but it doesn't align with empirical science.

# Timeless Pattern

To discover a time sequence, you need to think beyond time.

# Timeless Pattern

The riddle presents a scenario where a group of four people is being pursued by a horde of savage zombies. To escape, the four individuals must cross a bridge and cut its ropes before the zombies catch up to them. However, the zombies are quick and can reach them in just 17 seconds. Therefore, the group must all cross the bridge within 17 seconds or less. Each individual has a specific crossing time: the young boy takes 1 second, the girl takes 2 seconds, the man takes 7 seconds, and the professor takes 12 seconds. Additionally, due to the darkness, they need to carry a lantern with them. The riddle asks for the proper way to cross the bridge before the zombies arrive.

Before reading the solution on the next page, try to figure out the correct answer by yourself, noting that there are no tricks in the question.

The first thing that might come to your mind is that the young man, who crosses the bridge in one second, must go every time with someone and bring the lamp back to save time. However, this is not the correct answer.

## The Solution

The first two people who should cross the bridge are the young man and the girl, carrying the lantern. It takes them two seconds. The young man then returns with the lantern in one second, making the total time three seconds. Next, the professor and the man form the second pair to cross with the lantern, taking 10 seconds. The total time becomes 13 seconds. We should not forget that the girl is on the other side, so she returns with the lantern in two seconds. Afterward, she and the young man cross in two seconds as well, resulting in a total time of 17 seconds. Hence, they will be able to cross the bridge before the zombies arrive.

## How to Approach Chronological Problems

When dealing with temporal sequences, the most straightforward method involves trying all possible orders randomly. Starting with any two individuals, you work your way through until you find the correct solution. However, this approach can be extremely time-consuming, especially when dealing with larger groups. For instance, if there were twenty people instead of four, the number of possible combinations would be exceedingly high. Thus, we need a more intelligent strategy than random trials.

Breaking free from time-sequential thinking is challenging, as time can act like a trap, holding us within its circle. To overcome this limitation, we must shift our perspective and consider the problem from a dimension where time does not exist. This is akin to an ant walking on a bicycle tire; from the ant's tiny viewpoint, it believes it must pass through points "1" and "2" to reach "3," forming a seemingly straight path. Similarly, our perception of time often compels us to move through events sequentially. To address chronological problems effectively, we need to liberate ourselves from this linear perspective and explore alternative approaches.

Breaking free from the mental constraints of time can be challenging, similar to how the ant in the figure is confined to sequential movement. However, the man in the above figure has the advantage of viewing all points directly, allowing him to place the ant on any of the "1", "2", or "3" points without being bound by chronological thinking. His perspective from the outside liberates him from the time sequence, enabling him to perceive the problem from a different angle. This shift in perspective is crucial to solving such difficulties effectively. It demonstrates the power of stepping back from the constraints of linear thinking, which can unveil the panoramic view and open up new possibilities.

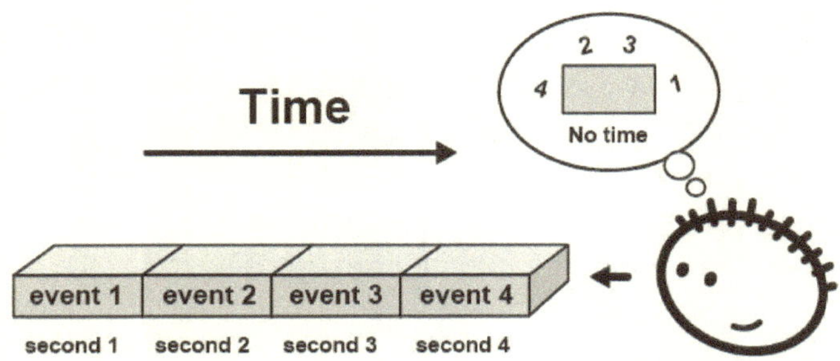


When we think beyond temporal contemplation, all occurrences appear to happen simultaneously, as portrayed in the illustration above. Imagine using cylindrical pieces instead of bricks; when observed sideways, a singular circle would manifest. For analysis purposes, we depict the circles intricately, as shown in the figure below. This shift in viewpoint empowers us to approach the quandary from a novel perspective, aiding in the discovery of the optimal solution.

## Riddle Solution Analysis

Riddle Solution: To solve this riddle, we need to reorder the events based on their importance rather than their chronological sequence. Our goal is to minimize the overall time taken. The most significant time reduction happens when a longer-duration event encompasses a shorter-duration event. For instance, to minimize time, it is crucial that the professor accompanies the man, effectively eliminating the man's seven-second crossing time. The overlapping sequence will appear as depicted below.

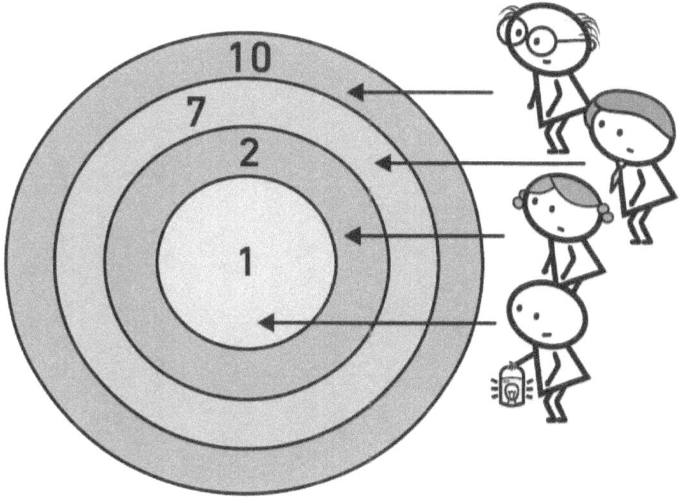


As a result, the girl and the boy must cross the bridge together. These two groups will take a total of 12 seconds to cross. This answers the question of who should go with whom. The next question is about who should bring the lantern back. In this case, the priority is reversed. The most important event now becomes the one that takes the least time to return. Therefore, group A (boy-girl) should be the one to return with the lantern, as group B has a longer return time. The analysis indicates that group A must cross first, allowing the young man to return with the lantern in three seconds. Subsequently, group B crosses in ten seconds. For the return, priority is given to the girl, who returns in two seconds, rather than the members of group B. Finally, group A crosses again in two seconds, resulting in a total time of 17 seconds.

As we mentioned, in dealing with temporal problems and ordering events, it is essential to move away from considering time as the primary factor and instead focus on "priority based on logic." In the previous example, the formation of two distinct groups (one for minimizing crossing time and the other for efficient return) inherently leads to the required time ordering. By replacing the sole consideration of time with logical prioritization, we arrive at an efficient solution to such temporal problems.

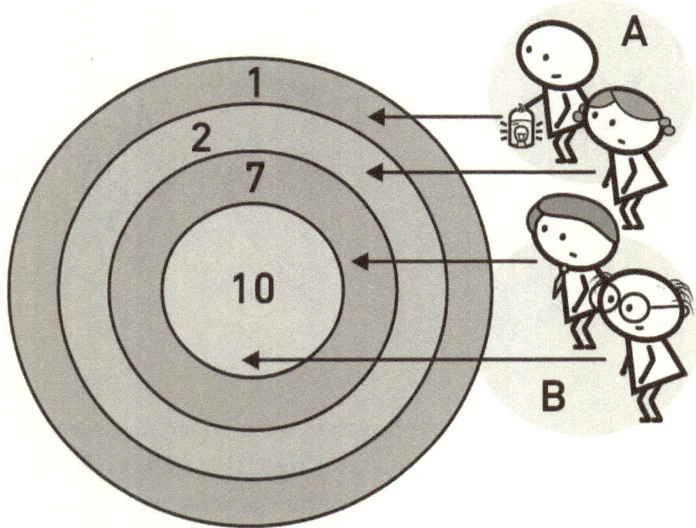


## Algorithms

An algorithm refers to a set of step-by-step instructions designed to accomplish a specific task, much like the steps found in a food recipe. We will explore the meaning of algorithms through the following story:

Late at night, in the darkness, a little boy finds himself alone on the bank of the river. Knowing that wild predators might approach, such as wolves, the boy must quickly build a strong high stand to hike until daylight.

You stand on the other side of the river, and both you and the child are unable to see anything due to the darkness. The boy has seven different-sized tree trunks by his side. His task is to stack these wooden trunks in order, from the largest to the smallest, to create a stable platform to climb on. The boy can only compare two trunks at once. Fortunately, you can help him with verbal instructions to arrange the trunks. What can you say to guide him?

## The solution

If you've ever tried to compare multiple objects in the dark, you'll know how difficult this is. However, comparing only two items at a time is doable.

To arrange the trunks from the largest one to the smallest, we need to follow a specific series of steps. Solving this problem requires a different approach than simply thinking in a step-by-step sequence. Instead of focusing on the first and second steps, we should devise the right ranking strategy. One of the effective strategies is as follows:

1. Begin by comparing the first two nearby trunks and placing the larger one on the right side.

2. Continue this process with the second and third trunks, and so on, until you reach the end of the trunks.

3. Once you have completed the first pass, start again from the beginning and repeat the process until no further rearrangements are needed.

You can guide the child to perform this strategy, as shown in the figure below. By following these steps, he will successfully sort all the trunks from the largest to the smallest to climb them.

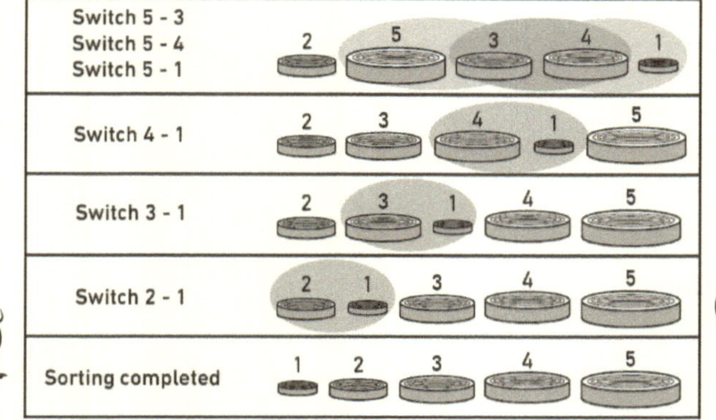

The strategy of "always putting the largest piece to the right" ensures that all the trunks are sorted, allowing the child to stack them and climb up to safety. This method is commonly known as the "bubble sort algorithm." The term "Algorithm" is credited to the Persian scientist Al-Khwarizmi, who lived during the 9th century. Algorithms are widely used in computer programming, where a series of particular precise commands are given to the machine to reach a solution step by step. It is critical to remember that you can't come up with the right algorithm "series of actions" by thinking within the timeline.

"An algorithm is a finite sequence of rigorous, well-defined instructions, typically used to solve a class of specific problems or to perform a computation." (Merriam-Webster Dictionary).

An informal definition of an algorithm can be described as "a set of rules that precisely define a sequence of operations." This encompasses all computer programs and any prescribed bureaucratic procedures or cook-book recipes. For instance, the step-by-step instructions on how to make a pancake represent an example of an algorithm.

The word "Algorithm" is derived from the name of the 9th-century Persian mathematician Muḥammad ibn Mūsā al-Khwārizmī (780–850). He was a versatile scholar who excelled in mathematics, astronomy, geography, and other fields. Al-Khwarizmi worked at the House of Wisdom in Baghdad, which was a renowned center of knowledge during that era. The term "Algorithm" emerged from his name when his Arabic treatise on the Hindu–Arabic numeral system was translated into Latin during the 12th century. The manuscript started with the phrase "Dixit Algorizmi" (Thus spake Al-Khwarizmi), leading to the adoption of the term "Algorithm." He became widely known in Europe during the late Middle Ages, primarily through another of his books, "The Algebra." His contributions to mathematics and science have had a lasting impact on human knowledge and problem-solving techniques.

## A Recipe for Spicy Salmon

Cooking recipes provide an excellent example of an algorithm, comprising step-by-step procedures. Let's explore the process of making spicy salmon:

## Steps:

1. Preheat the oven to 200°C.
2. Cover the baking dish with aluminum foil.
3. Prepare a thick paste by mixing garlic powder, chili pepper powder, olive oil, mustard, lime juice, salt, and pepper. Rub the salmon fillets with this paste.
4. Bake the salmon in the preheated oven for 15 minutes.
5. Check the salmon's flakiness with a fork; it's done when it flakes easily.

## Reverse Engineering

The algorithm described earlier is clear and simple to execute. However, it's important to recognize that in real-life situations, problems often don't come with pre-defined solutions. Consider a scenario where you encounter an already prepared salmon dish and wish to deduce the cooking processes used to create it. How can you devise an algorithm from a dish that's already been prepared?

To create an algorithm from a ready-made dish, you need to employ a reverse engineering approach. You'll need to analyze the dish's characteristics and use logical deduction to infer the likely cooking processes involved. For instance, if the salmon appears evenly cooked both inside and outside, it suggests that it wasn't subjected to prolonged heat exposure. Therefore, the oven might have been preheated before cooking. The flavor of the sauce could indicate whether it was marinated with the salmon before cooking. Additionally, the absence of sticking may suggest that the cooking surface was covered with a nonstick spray or baking sheet.

## The Nature of Time

The concept of "time" remains a mystery, yet its unidirectional flow is evident. To illustrate why time moves forward rather than backward, physicist Stephen Hawking presents a novel thought experiment: envision a glass cup on a table falling and shattering into pieces. While this is a familiar sight, we never observe the reverse, where shattered glass magically reassembles into an intact cup on the table. This phenomenon is attributed to the "law of entropy," which states that the universe tends to progress from order to disorder, not the other way around. Additionally, our psychological perception of time reinforces its forward motion, as we can recollect the past but not the future. Furthermore, the universe's ongoing expansion contributes to the unidirectional nature of time. In essence, reverse engineering provides a way to unravel solutions from existing outcomes, making it a valuable tool for problem-solving and innovation.

While the true nature of time remains elusive, its unidirectional aspect is undeniable. In this forward-time perspective, events unfold in a sequence, adhering to the law of causality, where event A causes event B, which leads to event C, and so forth.

Solving time-related problems within a time-based framework is akin to attempting to roll up a carpet while standing on it. To ease the process, it's better to step outside the carpet's boundaries to roll it up. Similarly, arranging events is more manageable when considering them from a perspective beyond the confines of time. In general, problems cannot be effectively solved within the context in which they arise.

A valuable piece of advice is encapsulated in the quote, "We cannot solve our problems with the same thinking we used when we created them," attributed to Albert Einstein. To successfully address the problem at hand, one must adopt a different perspective by mentally detaching themselves from the setting of the problem. Let's apply this approach to the following example:

## How to Organize Events Based on Logic?

In the scenario depicted above, we are presented with three images and tasked to determining the correct order of events. The first image "X" captures the

215

cup in the process of falling; the second image "B" shows the cup shattered into pieces; and the third image "D" displays a glass cup on a table. To organize these three images in the correct sequence, we can follow a logical approach based on physics.

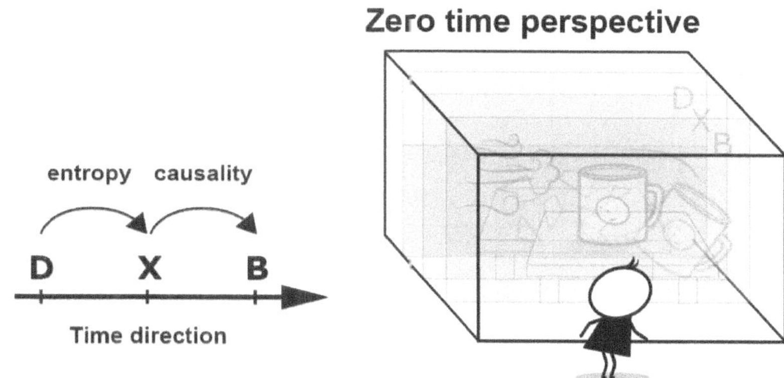



The law of causality indicates that the cup's fall is caused by the presence of air, suggesting that the air event must precede the cup falling. Additionally, the law of entropy tells us that a cup breaking into pieces is more probable than pieces coming together to form a whole cup. Hence, the scene of the fall must occur before the scene of the smashed cup.

* Causality refers to the relationship between cause and effect. It states that an event (cause) leads to another event (effect). While causality plays a significant role in understanding cause-effect relationships, it doesn't necessarily dictate the temporal order of events in all situations.

* Entropy is a concept from thermodynamics that measures the degree of disorder or randomness in a system. It tends to increase over time in closed systems, leading to the notion of the "arrow of time" where natural processes usually go from a state of lower entropy to a state of higher entropy. Also, applying entropy alone does not guarantee a unique chronological order of events in a given scenario.

Therefore, the correct order of events for the three imageries is as follows: Cup on table (D) → Cup falling (X) → Cup shattered (B). While not all event ordering issues can be resolved solely through causality and entropy logic, other logic constraints can provide valuable insights into deducing chronological sequences, as seen in the zombie riddle.

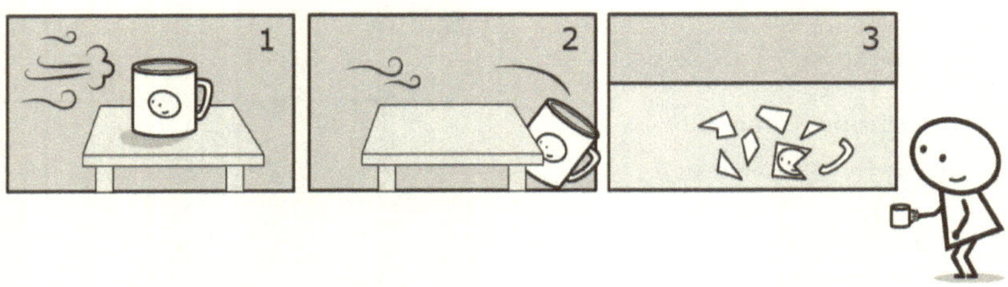

## Example 2

Let's consider a second example of a simple cooking scenario involving boiling water, adding pasta, and serving the cooked pasta. We will use the principles of entropy and causality to find the right chronological order of events.

Image A: The cooked pasta is served on a plate.
Image B: A pot of water on a stove, with a stove flame turned on.
Image C: The water in the pot is boiling vigorously.

Using entropy and causality logic, we can organize these images in the following chronological order:

Image B (Pot of water on a stove with the flame turned on) - Causality dictates that boiling water requires heat, so the water must be heated first before it can start boiling. Image C (Vigorously boiling water) - Entropy tells us that water tends to go from a lower energy state (cold water) to a higher energy state (boiling water) due to the application of heat. Image A (Cooked pasta served on a plate) - After the water has boiled, the pasta is added, cooked, and finally served on a plate. Therefore, the correct chronological order of events for this cooking scenario is: Image B → Image C → Image A.

## Summary

Chronological order refers to arranging events, actions, or information in the sequence they occurred, from earliest to latest, creating a timeline of events. It helps provide a clear and coherent understanding of the historical or temporal progression of a subject.

1. When tackling Chronological time-related problems, it is essential to think beyond the confines of the time dimension. That means, to arrange events in time, it is beneficial to disregard the time dimension and instead apply other alternative logical constraints.

2. In general, problems cannot be effectively solved by thinking within the same setting in which they originated.

3. Computer programs, also known as algorithms, consist of sequential instructions. Finding the appropriate algorithmic solution often requires thinking beyond a purely sequential approach.

# Control Pattern

Utilize the error to maintain the system's stability.

# Control Pattern

How does a young child learn to walk? Initially, the child has no idea where or how to place their feet. So they take an improvised initial step. When they stumble, they try to correct the error the next time by altering their step slightly and discovering the new outcome. The child repeats this practice over and over again, attempting to learn from their prior errors, until their ability to walk gradually improves and the errors fade away.

Children make major mistakes and fall a lot on their first steps. However, after a few years, these errors are reduced to minor ones. In engineering, this process of learning through trial and error is known as "Control Theory." Control theory gives rise to a comprehensive science known as "control engineering," which has numerous applications in various sectors of life. This pattern of error minimization can also be found in management, in the form of "quality control," and even in modern educational theories.

Control theory, as a way of thinking, is highly effective in situations where we are not entirely certain of what we are doing. For instance, if you plan to build a robot whose sole purpose is to pierce shirt buttons, and you have already calculated the exact force required to perforate the buttons and created the robot accordingly. In this scenario, we may not need to consider the control theory because we already know exactly what force value we require to do the job. However, in more complex and uncertain scenarios, where factors may change dynamically, control theory provides a valuable framework for adapting and achieving desired outcomes.

For the sake of argument, let's assume we are creating a walking robot. We have programmed it to walk uniformly, akin to the inexpensive toy robots found on the market. However, a problem arises when it stumbles over a small stone. The robot frequently falls due to a lack of "self-control" and "error correction." This is a classic scenario where the application of control theory becomes imperative.

Conversely, advanced robots constantly monitor their steps, and if an anomaly occurs, they adjust their steps to adapt, leveraging control theory to achieve self-balancing. Control theory is grounded in the recognition that we cannot predict the future. For instance, since the robot cannot anticipate the terrain it will traverse, it must improvise and learn from its errors as it progresses. When the robot stumbles, it employs the so-called "rule of subtraction" to calculate the necessary actions to restore its balance. This embodies the essence of control theory.

## A Robot That Can Improve its Walk

To build a robot that can improve its walk, we can utilize a liquid-based system with sensors. For instance, we employ water or any liquid inside the robot and use sensors to measure the water level at various corners. When the

robot is at rest (1: balanced), the water level remains horizontal, and there is no response. As the robot walks on smooth ground (2: balanced), the water level remains flat as well. However, if the robot steps on a stone and starts to fall (3: stumbled), the water level rises on one side. The "sensor" detects this rise in water level and sends a command to the robot to restore its body's tilt and maintain steady walking (4: balanced).

For example, if the water rises three centimeters on the right side, the sensor instructs the robot to adjust its body by moving three centimeters to the left in order to regain balance. The water effectively guides the robot to maintain its balance when it is on the verge of falling. In mathematical terms, we can express this as (Error in balance = current position - normal position.) The robot utilizes this calculated error value to continuously rebalance itself while walking. This technology is known as "feedback control," and its block diagram is shown below.

The desired input can be likened to "the flat water level," and the feedback is akin to "the level of water when the robot stumbles." The difference between these two water levels (flat level - tilt level) represents the amount of error, which is used to restore the robot to its stable position by the controller. This process repeats continuously during the robot's walking to maintain its

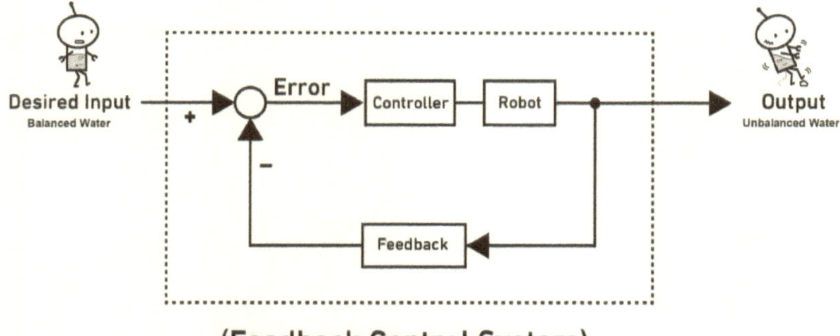


**(Feedback Control System)**

balance. It's important to note that when the robot is walking steadily, the output minus the input becomes zero, and the controller takes no action in this case, yet it keeps monitoring the walking cycle for any future incidents.

## Control Pattern in Biology:

In biology, every living organism possesses a system that maintains the body's equilibrium. This is achieved through steady internal physical and chemical states known as "homeostasis." For instance, the optimal body temperature is 37°C, and the ideal water percentage is about 50% of the body. When any disturbance occurs, the control mechanism comes into action to restore the body to its normal internal condition. This control system plays a crucial role in keeping our bodies within a healthy range.

Consider the scenario where you become extremely cold and your body responds by shivering to generate heat and return your body to its normal temperature. Similarly, when the body temperature increases, such as during physical exertion, the feedback control loop triggers sweating, which reduces the body temperature back to normal. This mechanism of control is referred to as a "negative feedback loop" because it aims to counteract any changes to the body's state.

On the other hand, in living beings, a "positive feedback loop" operates in the opposite direction. It amplifies changes rather than negating them. For instance, if you sustain an injury, a positive feedback control loop is activated, and the platelets in your blood detect the damaged location. They then cluster together and release chemicals to attract additional platelets, eventually leading to blood clotting and sealing the wounded vessel.

## Control Pattern in Management

The control pattern also appears in management science as "Quality Control." It involves a system or department responsible for maintaining the quality of products or services offered by a facility and correcting any deviations from the required standard. For instance, in a mobile phone manufacturing factory, if the management sets a standard that the battery should last for a full week, the quality department tests a sufficient sample of batteries to ensure they meet the criteria. If any defects are found, the batteries are remanufactured to restore compliance.

Broadly speaking, the control pattern is fundamental to management science, extending beyond just quality control. There are two main types of management: institutional management and project management. Both types require three essential components: an objective, a plan, and a method for handling deviations. As the plan is executed to achieve the goal, errors may occur, and it becomes the manager's role to identify and correct these faults.

"Risk management" is essentially a feedback control procedure involving some kind of pre-determined mini-plan that outlines how to deal with anticipated deviations and the necessary actions to restore alignment with the objectives. The management process can be compared to that of a shepherd controlling a flock of sheep, guiding wandering sheep back to their rightful positions based on a prepared plan to address potential escapes and appropriate corrective actions.

## Control Pattern in Education:

In the field of education, exams are used as a standardized way of assessing students' levels. However, some modern educational systems are evolving to view exams not only as a means of evaluation but also as a valuable source of feedback for students themselves. The philosophy behind this approach is that students must understand their mistakes during or after the exam in order to learn and improve continuously. This concept aligns with the philosophies of a feedback control system where the identification and analysis of mistakes act as catalysts for improvement.

According to a study by Hattie and Timperley (2007), providing effective feedback is essential for enhancing student learning. The study highlights that feedback that focuses on identifying errors and offering suggestions for improvement has a significant positive impact on students' academic performance. Another research in cognitive psychology, "The spacing effect", as demonstrated by Ebbinghaus (1885), suggests that learners retain information better when they revisit it after a certain period of time, allowing for errors to be corrected and knowledge to be reinforced.

In conclusion, the control pattern in education is not limited to traditional evaluations but also encompasses the utilization of exams and feedback as tools for continuous improvement and learning. By encouraging students to reflect on and learn from their mistakes, educational systems can enhance the learning process and foster greater academic achievement.

## The History of Control Theory

The origins of control theory can be traced back to Ctesiopius, who, around 250 B.C. in Alexandria, built the first autonomous machine—a water clock capable of maintaining a constant flow of water and correcting itself automatically. This innovation redefined the capabilities of machines, challenging the notion that only living beings could adapt their behavior to their surroundings.

Over time, other instances of autonomous technical devices emerged, such as James Watt's "steam engine controller" in the eighteenth century and Cornelis Drebbel's thermostat in the seventeenth century. In the nineteenth century, the mathematical foundations of self-balancing systems were established.

A significant figure in the development of control theory was Norbert Wiener (1894–1964), who laid down the principles of control theory as it is known today. Wiener believed that the distinguishing characteristic of living organisms is their ability to continuously reduce error. In control theory, "error" is defined as the difference between the current state and the desired state. Wiener's book, "Cybernetics," provided the foundational concepts and mathematical models of perception based on this definition. Additionally, Ross Ashby's book, "Design for a Brain" (1948–1952), contributed to the theory by defining intelligence as a feedback loop aimed at achieving balanced behavior.

Throughout history, enthusiasm for control theory has grown. Some scientists have even posited that it forms the basis of intelligent behavior in all living organisms, including humans. While control theory has shown its effectiveness in solving numerous problems, particularly through feedback cycles, it is important to acknowledge that it cannot fully replicate human intelligence.

## Control Theory Applications

The control pattern strategy finds applications in various fields, including engineering, biology, management, education, and others. It proves valuable in scenarios where problems may be addressed over time through iterations or in situations with uncertainty about the future, such as real-time systems. In both cases, the feedback loop is used to continually improve outcomes.

227

Although the control pattern may seem obvious, its significance remains profound, providing key solutions when dealing with uncertainty and ignorance about the future.

## Summary

The control pattern could be applicable in situations where:

b. There are upcoming future problems.
c. The desired ideal state is known and can be used as a reference point.

To implement the control pattern, follow these steps:

1. Define the equilibrium state of the system.
2. Measure the output value of the system.
3. Compare the output with the desired equilibrium state.
4. Utilize the difference, or "deviation," as feedback to restore the system's state.

# Unattainable Pattern

If the mountain is unreachable, you can still examine its shadow.

# Unattainable Pattern

Sometimes, the challenge is not merely difficult but rather unsolvable due to specific constraints. For example, determining the existence of life beyond our solar system is an unattainable problem because we lack the means to reach those distant planets or observe them through telescopes to search for signs of life. Our current technology simply cannot bridge this gap.

Another example of an unattainable problem is the mind-body problem. Some scientists argue that living beings, including humans, do not possess any spiritual qualities; rather, we are purely material bodies, and our conscious minds are merely by-products of the physical processes at work, akin to smoke emitting from a steam engine. According to this claim, there is no inner "soul" within us.

We will never know if aliens exist, because Mras is so far away

On the other hand, other researchers contend that the story of human existence goes beyond our physical makeup, and science has yet to identify the elusive quality that distinguishes us from inanimate objects like trees and rocks. The mind-body problem might eventually find a resolution through scientific exploration, or it might remain an unattainable challenge, at least for the so-called objective science.

When faced with such challenging problems, some may acknowledge, "We can't solve this for now, but perhaps in the future." They accept the current limitations and halt their efforts. However, great minds do not give up easily, even when confronted with seemingly insurmountable obstacles. Instead of accepting defeat, they persist in their quest and seek alternative approaches. They firmly believe that even if they cannot directly explore the mountain's peak, they can still examine its shadow.

## Can Computers Ever Reach Human Intelligence?

The unattainable problem we are going to discuss is related to Artificial Intelligence (AI). The question of whether computers can achieve true intelligence has been a topic of debate among scientists since the early days of computing. The problem with this question is that no one knows what intelligence really is. Is a dog more intelligent than a cat? How can we determine that? And what about a parrot? Is it more intelligent than both? Answering these questions is difficult because there is no universally accepted definition of intelligence.

We cannot determine with high certainty whether a cat is less intelligent than a parrot. For the fact that we can't tell what is going on inside the head of a cat or a parrot. Perhaps the thoughts of cats are more deep and wise than we assume. To address this question, the renowned scientist Alan Turing proposed a brilliant workaround to assess whether computers can be as intelligent as humans.

Before reading further, I encourage you to try for a moment to think of possible solutions or philosophies to address the question:

(Can computers become as smart as humans?)

## Turing's Solution

Turing drew inspiration from a British game known as the "Imitation Game," where a man and a woman hide behind a curtain, and the man attempts to pretend to be a woman. An interrogator's task is to discern between the actual woman and the pretending man through written questions.

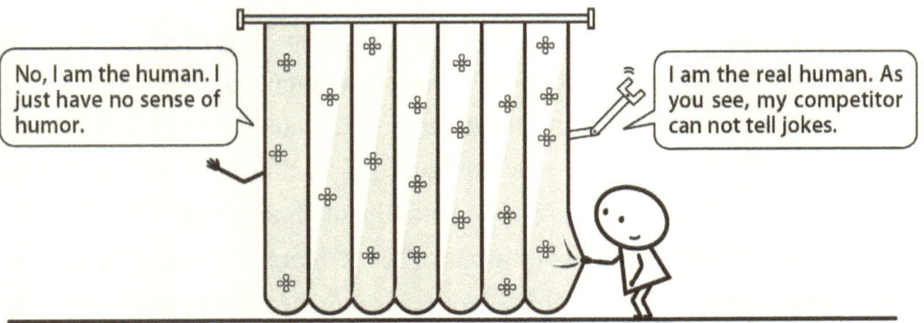


Turing adapted this game idea to measure computer intelligence. In the Turing test, there are three participants: a person, a machine, and an interrogator. The interrogator's goal is to distinguish between the real person and the computer. During the game, the computer attempts to persuade the interrogator that it is a human, while the human player aims to convince the interrogator that they are the genuine human. If the interrogator cannot determine which one is the real person within a set time, it is concluded that "this machine is as intelligent as a human."

Alan Turing recognized the complexities of defining intelligence and how it operates within our minds. Thus, he devised a brilliant workaround that simplifies the process of judging the intelligence of a computer.

You can see how simple and beautiful Turing's solution to "defining intelligence" is. The elegance of his approach lies in avoiding a direct definition of intelligence and instead focusing on the observable behavior of an intelligent person. This "Turing test" remains relevant today as a means to assess a computer system's intelligence. Remarkably, no computer has ever passed the Turing test to date. Nonetheless, the Turing test played a pivotal role in establishing the field of Artificial Intelligence, laying its foundations, and inspiring thousands of scientists and researchers to push the field of AI forward.

Indeed, there have been doubts about Turing's definition of intelligence using the "imitation game" method. However, given that we lack a solid definition of "intelligence," we should accept Turing's test as the best workaround available. It represents the most suitable approach for assessing something without defining its nature, as it focuses solely on external behavior. Moreover, it introduces a novel thinking technique to learn.

There is a well-known joke about a clown who lost his wallet in his house. Faced with darkness inside, he opts to search for it on the street under a streetlamp where visibility is better. While this serves as a humorous anecdote, it also reflects an intriguing concept. Imagine a house that is

234

completely inaccessible. In such a scenario, the most ingenious approach to uncovering its mysteries would involve examining its reflection on the wet street or in the windows of neighboring houses.

In conclusion, the quest to determine whether computers can attain human-like intelligence remains a fascinating and challenging endeavor. Turing's test offers a valuable perspective on evaluating intelligence, even in the absence of a definitive definition.

## Summary

1. When severe limitations restrict our ability to find a solution, we shouldn't abandon the pursuit; instead, we can explore the problem's reflection, shadow, or behavior.

2. Even though analyzing the reflection of a problem might not resemble examining the original problem, it is still better than having no solution at all.

3. Problems that lie beyond the scientific realm can still be approached scientifically using this behaviorism approach.

# Heavens Pattern

If something appears in two different places at once, then it doesn't exist yet.

# Heavens Pattern

In 1801, the British scientist Thomas Young conducted an important experiment known as the "Double-slit experiment." During this experiment, Young directed a beam of light onto a plate that contained two thin slits. According to the prevailing view of light at the time, it was believed to consist of particles, a concept developed by Newton.

The expected outcome was that the light would appear on the facing wall as two lines, one for each slit, as each slit would output a separate beam of light. However, the actual result was quite unexpected. Instead of just showing two lines, a series of multiple lines appeared on the wall.

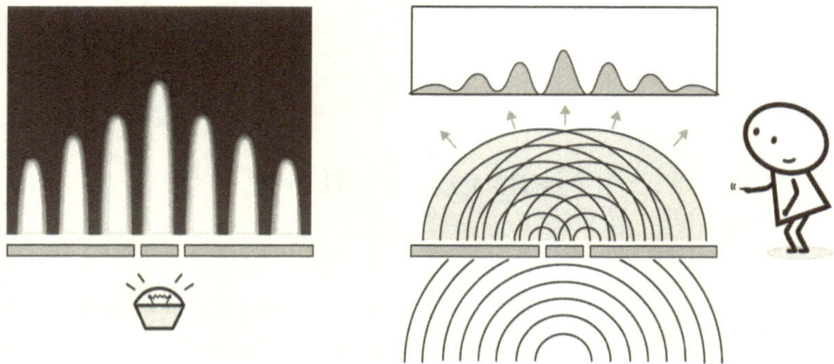

Light and water behave similarly when meet a barrier with two slots.

Young's experimental findings challenged the particle theory of light and led to another interpretation. In his book "Experiments and Calculations Relative to Physical Optics," published in 1803, he explained why the light appeared on the wall in several lines instead of just two. This groundbreaking work contributed significantly to the understanding of light and laid the foundation for the wave theory of light. Young's insights marked a pivotal moment in the history of science, reshaping our understanding of light's behavior and the fundamental principles that govern it.

Young used a tank filled with water, as shown in the first figure, to explain the phenomenon in the following manner:

"When a stone is thrown into the water, it creates circular waves, as depicted in the figure. Furthermore, if a wooden barrier with two holes is placed in the middle of the tank, small circular waves emerge from each hole on the opposite side of the tank. When these two waves meet, they interfere with each other, leading to the formation of a larger wave that is higher in the middle and lower on the sides, as illustrated on the right side of the tank. This resulting wave is known as the interference wave."

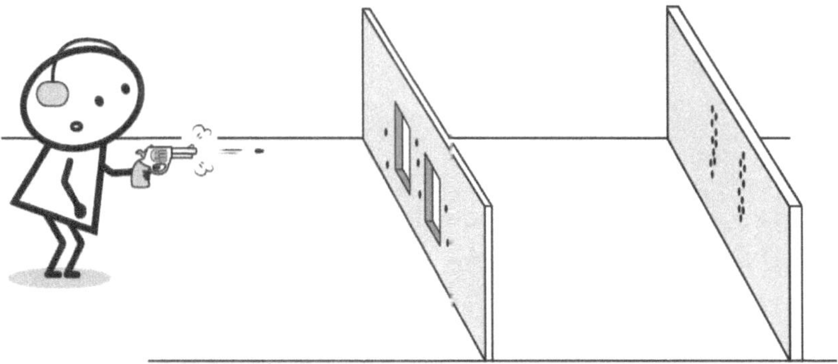

From the water experiment, Young inferred that when light passes through a barrier with two slits, it generates two overlapping waves, similar to the water waves. This led him to conclude that light cannot be composed of microscopic particles, as was previously believed, because if it were, it would only appear on the wall as two lines. Therefore, Young proposed that light must travel in waves similar to water waves.

However, this conclusion led to a perplexing problem for scientists. To better understand this issue, let's consider what would happen if we repeated the experiment using gun bullets instead of water.

When gun bullets, which are distinct entities, pass through the barrier with two slits, they would leave two columns of holes on the right wall, as shown in the figure above. This is understandable and follows the classical notion of particles behaving as particles.

In 1961, a German scientist named Claus Jönsson conducted an experiment similar to the bullet experiment, but he used electrons instead. Jönsson employed an electron microscope gun to fire only one electron particle at a time towards the two slits. Surprisingly, unlike the bullet experiment, the outcome resembled the water wave experiment. The shape of interference waves appeared on the wall instead of two columns, which was bizarre and incomprehensible.

The peculiar part is that electrons can be thought of as little balls, and each electron should pass through one of the two slits, either the right or the left slit. It seems nonsensical for an electron to pass through both slits simultaneously. For instance, if you consider your cat entering the house, it can choose to use either the front door or the back door. It cannot possibly enter the house through both doors at the same time unless it were a ghost cat. However, the electron exhibits this seemingly contradictory behavior.

In 2013, at the University of Nebraska, a team led by "Roger Bach" conducted the double-slit experiment again with electrons. They shot only one electron at a time with great precision and observed the experiment for two hours. Over time, the wall displayed the interference pattern of many columns, indicating that electrons behaved like waves when passing through the two slits. Remarkably, this experiment applies not only to electrons but also to photons or even atoms, suggesting that the wave-particle duality phenomenon is a general characteristic of both light and matter.

However, scientists were bothered by the double-slit experiment because they wanted to determine precisely which slit the electron passes through. To address this question, they introduced a camera near the two slits to monitor the electron's behavior as it approached them. Surprisingly, when the slits were observed, each electron went through one of the slits normally, akin to bullets passing through distinct holes. Consequently, the wall displayed two normal columns of electrons, and the interference wave vanished. This observation illustrates the profound influence of the act of observation on the behavior of particles at the quantum level, raising questions about the nature of reality and the role of consciousness in shaping our the universe.

This peculiar outcome can be compared to installing two cameras, one at your house's front door and one at the back door. In the video footage, the cat seems to enter the house through the front door normally, and nothing unusual occurs. However, when the cameras are removed, you find the cat's footprints leading through both the front and back doors simultaneously, appearing at the very same moment. The cat seems to have entered through both doors at once, which defies our intuition and understanding of how things work. It appears impossible, yet it is also the truth revealed by the experiment.

As we all know, nothing can pass through two doors at the same time. Nonetheless, the double-slit experiment challenges this intuitive knowledge, making it one of the strangest experiments ever conducted in the history of science; with no solid and easily understandable explanation. The wave-particle duality observed in this experiment remains a fascinating and perplexing aspect of quantum mechanics.

This phenomenon highlights the enigmatic nature of the quantum world and the limits of our classical understanding when faced with the weirdness of subatomic behavior. The door for new interpretations is still open for curious minds to tackle the problem and contribute their ideas and perspectives to shed more light on the subject.

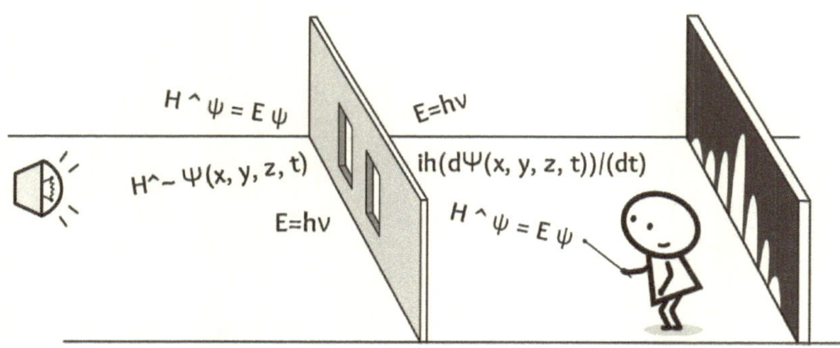


## The Proposed Solution

The logical solution lies in understanding that at the quantum level, particles like electrons and photons do not behave in the same way as macroscopic objects in our everyday experience. Classical mechanics, which governs the behavior of larger objects, does not apply at the quantum level.

Today, the explanation that many scientists adopt to elucidate the double-slit experiment is known as "The Copenhagen Interpretation." This conceptual framework was developed by a group of scientists led by Niels Bohr and Werner Heisenberg.

According to this interpretation, the electron does not possess a definite, real existence prior to observation; instead, it is described as a statistical probability distribution spread out in space. The electron (or photon) only manifests and comes into existence when it interacts with the screen at the end of the experiment. In other words, as the electron approaches the two slits, it does not divide into two separate electrons or transform into a wave. In reality, there is no real "physical" electron present in space at that moment; there exists only a "mathematical probability" associated with the electron's behavior. This mathematical probability distribution is akin to what a wave passing through the slits would create, ultimately registering as a single point on the end wall when measured or observed. The Copenhagen Interpretation provides a way to understand the peculiar behavior of particles at the quantum level, though it challenges our classical intuitions about the nature of reality.

I hope you can see the peculiarity of this reasoning. According to the Copenhagen Interpretation, the particles comprising our universe are not inherently real all the time; rather, they exist as mere mathematical probabilities without any physical presence. The world seemingly pops into existence as a result of these calculations. For instance, at a particular moment, there might be no actual electron or atom; there would only be probabilistic values. This is comparable to a scenario where a cat has a 30% chance of entering through the front door and a 70% chance of entering through the kitchen door, and at that moment, there is no tangible cat, just the probability. However, the moment someone looks to check the cat's location, it instantaneously appears from nowhere into existence at the front door.

This cat metaphor is just an illustration, as this phenomenon does not occur in macroscopic entities like cats, cars, or humans. It is characteristic of subatomic particles such as electrons, photons, and even atoms.

While you might not encounter situations like the "double-slit" problem in your daily life or consider the Copenhagen Interpretation as the definitive answer to the quantum mechanics phenomena, it is a powerful thinking technique that can boost your cognitive faculty and push the boundaries beyond conventional thinking. When an entity exhibits ghost-like behavior, seemingly existing in multiple places simultaneously, the Copenhagen interpretation becomes applicable. In this view, this entity is nothing more than mathematical probabilities at a specific moment, and it only emerged as a real entity when observed or measured.

244

This philosophical approach is known as "Epistemology," which explores knowledge as the origin of reality. It contrasts with "ontology," that concerned with studying what truly exists in the world and then deriving knowledge from these existing elements.

In conclusion, the logical solution to the double-slit experiment lies in accepting the peculiar nature of quantum mechanics, where particles exhibit both wave-like and particle-like behavior, and observation plays a crucial role in determining their behavior. Although challenging to reconcile with classical intuitions, this aspect of quantum physics is well-established and experimentally verified.

If the Copenhagen Interpretation holds true, it implies that reality is nothing but a ghostly probability, where the physical world emerges from the realm of possibilities when observed or measured.

## Summary

Although you may not encounter situations where you can apply this thinking pattern, it is still valuable to exercise your intelligence by contemplating such rare cases.

1. When we cannot precisely determine the state or condition of something, it may be considered unreal at that moment and only becomes real when we interact with it.

2. Certain systems can be visualized as a cloud of probability with no real physical existence. This probability collapses into a definite physical state when subjected to observation or measurement.

3. Nothing can physically go through two doors simultaneously unless it exists as an abstracted mathematical concept.

# Metaphor Pattern

Extend any law beyond its literal sense.

# Metaphor Pattern

Metaphorical thinking stands out as the most advanced thinking style presented in this book. It enables us to transcend the literal applications of the twenty patterns discussed earlier. By utilizing verbal metaphors, we can adapt and apply these patterns in unconventional situations. Take the Trojan horse pattern, for instance, which originally revolves around infiltrating a fortress and conquering it from within by adopting the guise of an object that smoothly integrates into the fortified system. Through the power of metaphor, we can extend this pattern to a broader and more abstract context.

Imagine the following scenario: A mother wants to teach her child mathematics, but the child strongly dislikes sitting down for formal lessons and shows no interest in math. Despite trying various methods to motivate him, nothing seems to work, and he continues to resist arithmetic lessons.

However, the mother notices that her child is enthusiastic about computer games. Inspired by this, she decides to introduce a math-based video game that teaches mathematics while engaging in play. In doing so, she applies the metaphorical thinking approach to transform the traditional method of teaching into an enjoyable and interactive learning experience for her child.

Indeed, the mother employed the Trojan horse strategy once again, but this time in a conceptual rather than physical manner. The impenetrable stronghold represents the child's aversion to mathematics on a psychological level. When we directly confront this resistance, the child's reaction is to push back even harder. Instead, the most effective approach is to discover the metaphorical Trojan horse, something that the child embraces and welcomes wholeheartedly, like "video games." Once identified, we can then endeavor to infuse educational value into this preferred medium.

## About the Original Troy Story

Upon closer examination of the origin story of the Trojan horse, we realize that it goes beyond a mere physical occurrence. When we attempt to breach the fortress door forcefully, a physical reaction repels us. However, the ultimate solution was not purely physical but rather had a psychological side, as the Romans seduced the Trojans with fake booties. Hence, the hack involves a blend of both physical and psychological elements.

## Pattern of Patterns (Metaphor)

The concept of "patterns of the patterns" explores the idea of constructing intricate physical entities through the arrangement of simple nested shapes. For instance, a complex mountain could be formed by repeatedly dividing simple triangles into smaller triangles.

Metaphorically, this pattern could be rephrased as "complex structures may arise from a single nested concept." These structures may take various forms, ranging from physical to mental, or even something in between.

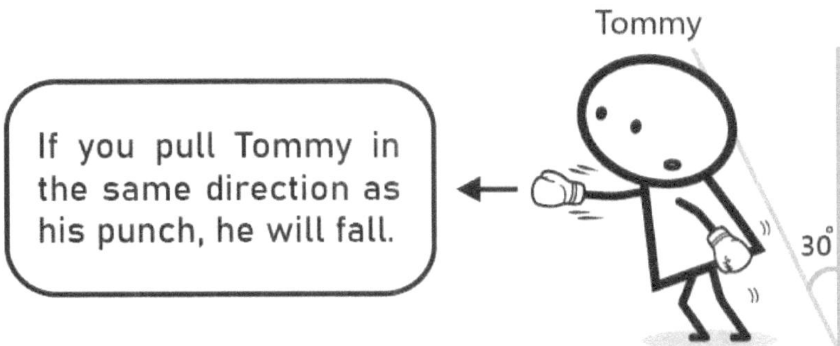


Another metaphorical example of employing the Trojan horse technique to achieve a non-physical penetration goal can be found in certain self-defense tactics.

Take the martial art of "Judo" which translates to "the gentle way" in Japanese, as an illustration. In this discipline, victory in combat is attained by utilizing the opponent's weight and strength as weapons against them while conserving one's own physical and mental energy. Judo exemplifies the idea that intelligence surpasses raw power. The technique involves initially gripping the opponent, off-balancing them by redirecting their momentum, and finally pinning them to the ground.

In a metaphorical sense, our goal to "defeat our opponent and pin him to the ground" can be interpreted as a physical protected area. The opponent will naturally resist any attempts to be defeated. Once we have both the protected area and the resistance, the Trojan horse technique can be applied.

Cleverly, we may easily induce our opponent to fall down by pulling them in the same direction as their strike, using their own weight and momentum against them.

While Judo's primary objective is somewhat physical, there is no "closed area" to break into, as seen in the traditional Trojan pattern. However, we can metaphorically consider the "closed area" as "refusing to fall on the ground," and the opposing reaction equivalent as "your opponent's force and weight."

* Note: This example is only a simplification. In Judo, you wouldn't typically "pull" an opponent's punch. Instead, you might use their momentum against them through techniques like throws or sweeps, but it requires proper timing, positioning, and technique execution.

## Summary

Through metaphorical thinking, we can expand most of the thinking patterns we've learned to encompass more diverse and general situations. Employing metaphors allows us to express these methods in a way that transcends specific instances.

**Example: generalizing the Trojan horse pattern metaphorically:**

1. The Trojan horse pattern can be metaphorically described as "overcoming any form of resistance, whether physical or psychological, by utilizing the reaction to our advantage."

   Consequently, the Trojan horse method transcends its original historical context of penetrating a besieged city. Instead, it can be adapted to delve into an individual's mind to achieve various objectives, such as education or rehabilitation. In this analogy, the besieged city represents an "isolated human psyche."

2. Symbolically, each thinking pattern —with the right abstraction—has the potential to be effective in physical situations, conceptual situations, or a combination of both. Metaphorical thinking broadens the scope of these patterns, making them applicable in diverse scenarios and contexts.

# Combining Thinking Tactics

Example: Use Thinking Tactics in Education

# Combining Thinking Tactics

Example: Combining Thinking Tactics to Enhance Education

We have discovered twenty-one different thinking patterns So far. You can substantially boost your thinking power if you mix some of those thinking approaches. For example, what will happen if we combine the "pattern of patterns" with the pattern of "control"? Or the pattern of "Mechanics" with the pattern of "Heart"? This convergence will lead to endless possibilities. In the pursuit of creating the finest education system for our children, we can employ various thinking tactics to enhance the learning experience.

Self-Realization (Belief Pattern)
Encourage students to embrace their true identities and believe in their potential. When they see themselves as engineers, writers, artists, or scientists, they are more likely to excel in those fields. Learning becomes a self-realization activity, where students naturally gravitate towards subjects that align with their personalities. As educators, it is crucial to tailor the educational content to resonate with each learner's unique identity, leading to better learning outcomes.

Touching the Ground (Belief Pattern)
Start lessons with familiar and relatable concepts to provide a solid foundation for learning. By beginning with well-known naive facts, stories, and everyday situations, students feel grounded and comfortable before diving into more

complex topics. Avoid using overly complicated language, as it may create barriers to understanding.

The Heart Arrow (Heart Pattern)
One word can translate into tremendous amount of knowledge; when experienced educators passionately convey their knowledge, it reaches the hearts of learners. Simple yet heartfelt expressions can deliver profound insights and understanding. A single heartfelt phrase can convey more than countless pages of textbooks. Cultivate a genuine connection with students through to inspire and empower their learning journey.

Mechanical Models (Mechanics Pattern)
Science endeavor is nothing but an attempt to find a mechanistic description of the world. Translate abstract concepts into tangible mechanical models to make learning more accessible, especially for younger learners. Humans are naturally inclined to understand physical objects better than abstract ideas. Utilize mechanical depictions and visual aids to facilitate comprehension and retention of complex topics.

Use Mistakes (Control Pattern)
Emphasize the importance of mistakes in the learning process. Mistakes are not failures but essential stepping stones to progress. Encourage students to embrace their mistakes as opportunities for growth and learning. Similarly as a toddler learns to walk by stumbling and correcting, students can enhance their understanding through the "mistakes/correct" cycle.

Fluency (Heart Pattern)
Promote repetition and practice to develop fluency in learned concepts. Mastery takes time and practice, just like an acrobat perfecting their juggling routine. Allow learners to engage in repeated exercises and discussions to achieve a deeper level of understanding and spontaneity in their knowledge.

By integrating these thinking tactics into education, we can create a dynamic and empowering learning environment. Students will not only gain knowledge but also develop a deeper understanding of themselves and their potential. As educators, let us explore the possibilities of combining these thinking patterns to shape the future of education for the better.

Using the aforementioned patterns to enhance education and syllabuses would transform the learning process and augment learners' understanding.

# Conclusion

The patterns of thinking presented in this book have been collected over an extended period from various sources and subjective experiences. While they are still far from being perfect or complete, my hope is that they will promote your problem-solving abilities and creativity. Combining all of these patterns into a single universal thinking method remains elusive at this point, as the sciences have not yet reached a horizon of consilience. However, if any law ever can connect these patterns, I can find no better than the wisdom: "Things always lead to their opposites." Often, the finest answers emerge from the least expected places.

## Thinking Tactics Summary:

When confronting a system, the 'Trojan horse' strategy of going along with it to avoid opposition might be the most suitable option, whether the system is physical or mental in nature.

In situations where maximizing returns requires utilizing specific resources, thinking 'Out of the box' becomes necessary. Consider the highly unlikely outcomes and whether the solution lies within the very question.

The 'Scientific' thinking pattern indicates that some problems can be directly solved through reasoning, with no need for workarounds. The key is to connect argument pieces logically to arrive at a valid solution, ensuring objectivity, consistency, and uninterrupted linkage.

The 'Google pattern' reveals the unity of sciences and how solutions can be found in different domains of knowledge. Borrowing ideas from unrelated fields can lead to innovative solutions. This concept highlights the importance of interdisciplinary thinking and the potential for breakthroughs when ideas intersect across diverse areas of expertise.

The 'Inverted sock pattern' suggests that sometimes the problem lies in our perspective of the world. By reinventing our worldview, we may find solutions that were previously hidden from us.

When studying a problem that surpasses scientific bounds due to constraints, considering it an 'Unattainable' pattern might prompt us to find reflections, shadows, or behaviors of the problem to act upon instead, leading to second-degree solutions.

The 'Heart pattern' emphasizes the importance of human-related patterns. By triggering specific emotions and feelings, we can tap into our practical knowledge and abilities.

The 'Belief pattern' also focuses on human behavior, emphasizing the role of faith and conviction in inspiring change. Convincing someone of the 'why' can be more effective in bringing about change than simply telling them 'what' to do.

In the 'Control pattern,' feedback loops play a crucial role in maintaining stability and desired outcomes in systems, be it in management, education, treatment, or engineering.

The 'Hidden dimension pattern' suggests that when faced with a deadlock, the solution might exist in another dimension or perspective, beyond our current understanding.

The 'Poetry pattern' highlights the human aspect of creativity and literary expression, emphasizing the importance of honest emotions in creating masterpieces.

The 'Timeless pattern' teaches how to handle problems involving sequences of actions by rising above time and applying logic constraints to identify the correct sequence of steps.

In the 'Pattern of patterns,' complexity can often be broken down into simple, self-similar patterns nested within each other, like a mountain made up of repeated basic patterns.

The 'Mechanics pattern' encourages visualizing and understanding problems through mechanical representations, even in fields that aren't purely mechanical, as it aids prediction and analysis.

The 'Einstein pattern' emphasizes mental experiments and imagination to reach novel conclusions, especially when faced with unusual or counterintuitive phenomena.

The 'Probability pattern' deals with forecasting the future based on probabilistic maps, acknowledging the limitations of exact equations.

The 'Opposites pattern' reveals the interconnectedness of polar opposites, allowing us to understand one half by discovering its opposite.

The 'Goat pattern' relates to statistical quandaries, emphasizing the importance of tracking and accounting for our ignorance in probability-based problems.

The 'Contradiction pattern' explores how logical inconsistencies can be used to disprove something's existence or halt a system's operation.

The 'Heaven pattern' provides a sophisticated and abstract interpretation of reality, useful for investigating unique and paradoxical behaviors.

The final pattern, the 'Metaphor pattern,' allows us to transcend and generalize the other patterns using verbal metaphors in various contexts.

The nature of thinking remains mysterious, with no definitive understanding of where our best ideas originate. Science outlines what excellent thinking should achieve, but the underlying mechanisms within the brain remain unclear.

Despite this uncertainty, the twenty-one thinking patterns offer valuable guidance, and they can be combined like Lego bricks to create new and complex thinking tactics for problem-solving, creativity, and intellectual endeavors. Embracing these patterns opens up endless possibilities for growth and exploration.

**Thinking Tactics**
A Journey in the Human Mind

www.ingramcontent.com/pod-product-compliance
Lightning Source LLC
Chambersburg PA
CBHW051249250726
48656CB00004B/1209